CW00552428

The Fighting Cameliers

The Fighting Cameliers

The Exploits of the
Imperial Camel Corps in the
Desert and Palestine Campaigns
of the First World War

Frank Reid

LEONAUR

The Fighting Cameliers: the Exploits of the Imperial Camel Corps in the Desert and Palestine Campaigns of the First World War
by Frank Reid

Copyright © 1934 Frank Reid

Published by Leonaur Ltd

Material original to this edition
copyright © 2005 Leonaur Ltd

ISBN (10 digit): 1-84677-035-1 (hardcover)
ISBN (13 digit): 978-1-84677-035-7 (hardcover)

ISBN (10 digit): 1-84677-025-4 (softcover)
ISBN (13 digit): 978-1-84677-025-8 (softcover)

http://www.leonaur.com

Publisher's Notes

Chapter 1

When four long lines of khaki-clad men lined up one morning early in 1916 at Abbassia, on the outskirts of Cairo, and stood in readiness to receive their first training in handling and riding camels, not one of them had any idea what lay before him. Many had transferred into the newly-formed Camel Corps at Tel-el-Kebir a few weeks previously because they resented the monotonous hours of drilling on the dry and burning sands fringing the Suez Canal.

Most of these men were Gallipoli veterans. After keeping the Turks at bay on the rugged and shell-torn slopes of Anzac for long weary months, they considered that on their return to Egypt after the evacuation, they should have been allowed to take things easy until further fighting was to be done. It was over the odds to expect them to take any interest in the same drill to which they had been accustomed before they received their baptism of fire on that narrow strip of land washed by the waters of the Aegean Sea. They had fought side by side with English regulars, and dark-skinned fighting men from India, and after a well-known English war correspondent had informed the world that they were the most reckless and daring fighters on Gallipoli, they formed the opinion, and broadcasted it far and wide that they were worthy of something better than marching across the historic old battlefield of Tel-el-Kebir with full packs, forming fours, and saluting by numbers. Such training was a dashed insult to Gallipoli veterans like themselves. They drilled and complained, and waited for something to happen.

When Sir Archibald Murray took over the command of the Eastern Expeditionary Force in January 1916, he realized that in the desert warfare ahead of him he would have to transport infantry from certain centres as speedily as possible; and that to do this he would require camels. Away back in the dim past the Persians, mounted on camels, had routed the horsemen of the Lydian hordes. Napoleon used camels in Egypt, and British Life Guards rode on them to the relief of Khartoum.

General Murray immediately thought of the Australians, recently returned from Gallipoli and bivouacked at Tel-el-Kebir. Here were men who could endure the hardships connected with desert fighting, and would excel in warfare in open country devoid of any shelter worth considering. He called for volunteers from brigades of the 1st and 2nd Australian Infantry Divisions. The result of the call was the formation of four companies, each consisting of six officers and a hundred and sixty-nine other ranks.

When routine orders, read out at Tel-el-Kebir one morning, announced that recruits were required for a Camel Corps about to be formed, the bored infantry men saw the opportunity for which they had waited so long. Once again they would be bivouacked near Cairo. Few of them knew anything about the habits of a camel, but they were confident that handling and riding the brutes could never be so monotonous as the infantry drill at which they had groused during the past few months.

It has been said that many of these men who enlisted in the first four companies of the Camel Corps were undesirables who were not required any longer in the battalions with which they had fought on the Peninsula. This may be true of a small section of the men, but not of the majority. When these were attached to the newly-formed unit, the battalions from which they were transferred lost some of the finest fighting men in the A.I.F. Subsequent events proved this.

Certainly there were some reckless characters amongst the men who went to Abbassia to become Cameliers; I doubt if so many "hard-doers" could have been found in any other Australian fighting unit. When Captain James Barber, adjutant of the newly-formed corps, and a typical dapper regular from an English mounted unit, stood and watched the men from Tel-el-

Kebir as they marched past the orderly room on their way to the newly-erected barracks at Abbassia, he turned to an English sergeant standing by his side and muttered:

"By gad, we're going to have trouble with those fellows."

His words were prophetic. During the weeks that followed hardly a day passed without at least half a dozen of the Cameliers being paraded at the orderly room for disorderly conduct. They added much to the gaiety of Cairo, and there were many wild escapades in which they took a leading part. The drivers and conductors of the white trams running from Cairo to Heliopolis suffered as much as anyone else. Nearly every night there was a stoppage of the service because the Cameliers would not pay their fares on the homeward journey. After a heated argument a conductor would be pushed off the tram and the driver would follow him. Then a volunteer driver from among the Cameliers would make a non-stop run to Abbassia. Those were wild rides, with gongs clanging as the trams proceeded full speed across intersections with natives, fowls, and donkeys scattering in all directions to escape injury. On leave in Cairo they became mixed up in cafe brawls, assaulted the Military Police, showed a decided reluctance to saluting officers, and in barracks even fought among themselves.

Soon after the Cameliers came to Abbassia I was attached to the orderly room staff. One morning when several of the men had to "toe the carpet" after a wild night in Cairo, Captain Barber turned to me.

"I say, Reid," he said, "are there still bushrangers in Australia?"

"No, sir," I replied.

"I quite believe you," he muttered grimly. "They've sent them all over here to join the bally Camel Corps."

Captain Barber never understood these tall, gaunt, and wiry Australians. They refused to take him seriously; rarely saluted him; and had a habit of giving him a nod or waving to him as they passed each other. One afternoon he returned from Cairo in a towering temper, stormed into the orderly room, and raved:

"It's over the bally odds, and I am going to stop it. Two hours ago I was passing Shepheard's when I met one of the confounded men from this Corps. He was drunk. Do you know what the infernal blighter did? Lurching up, he slapped me on the shoulder, and said, 'Hullo, old sport, what about having a drink with me?' Slake a crime-sheet out and have him placed under arrest as soon as he returns to barracks."

"His name, sir?"

"His name!" Repeated the irate officer. "Damn his name? How do I know his name? Make a crime-sheet out at once and don't ask damn fool questions."

I have already stated that when they first came to Abbassia few of these men knew anything about the habits of camels. Reinforcements who later joined the Corps were more fortunate in this respect. At Menangle Camp in New South Wales, Abdul Wade, the "camel king'" of Central Australia, had supplied the future Cameliers with four of these animals, and although not enough for actual Camel Corps work, they served at least to accustom the men to the smell, bad temper, and peculiar habits of the tricky brutes.

The first morning on parade at Abbassia the four newly-formed companies of Cameliers gazed at the animals in front of them with mixed feelings. A few hours previously one of the brutes had charged a Gyppo attendant and bitten through his skull. Back in one of the huts his dead body was then being prepared for burial. These camels had been brought from the Sudan; those issued to companies formed later, came from India, and were known as Bikanir camels. Those from the Sudan were of mixed colours, from white to smoky fawn, while all the Bikanirs were a red, sandy fawn. The Sudanese camels were much smarter, and quicker at moving than the others.

After staring for several minutes at one brute bubbling fretfully, a private in No 1 Company, who had been afraid of nothing on the Peninsula, turned to an English instructor standing near him.

"Hey, sergeant," he whispered, "pick me out a nice, quiet camel."

"Did you never ride a camel before?" Snapped back the non-com.

"No."

"Well," said the sergeant, pointing to a gaunt framed, wild-looking animal, standing with the others, "there's the camel for you, me lad. The Gyppos reckon he's never been ridden before, so you can start out together."

The first day's training provided these men of the 1st Camel Battalion with many opportunities for studying the queer ways of the animals that were to carry them over the desert sands of Egypt and Sinai during the long months that were ahead of them. Their first glance at the brutes was anything but reassuring. There was a supercilious, haughty expression of disdain about the hump-backed, splayed-footed, knock-kneed, long-necked, unwieldy creatures which chilled right from the beginning any feelings of intimacy that might be desired between a camel and his rider.

It took the new Cameliers some little time to discover and act upon the little weaknesses of the animals. A few looked no more ferocious than an angry bulldog that had gone hungry for a few days; but as a rule they seemed to regard everyone who approached them as a potential enemy, to be growled at, grunted at, and snapped at with an intensity of purpose that any tiger might well envy.

When I was introduced to the camel that was to be my property for the time being, I modestly retired, quelled by the fixed glare of contempt in its eyes; and when it reared itself from its haunches like a U-boat in a rough sea, and as daintily as an elephant dancing a two-step, I kept at a respectful distance lest I became engulfed in the upheaval.

We soon learned that the centre of attraction about the brutes was their teeth, and they knew it! They had a habit of displaying them on every possible occasion, probably to impress anyone uninterested with their business-like properties. Their lips hung leeringly down, smacking each other, and sometimes allowing a corner to droop just as if they were going to say something confidential. It was only a trick of his—(I say *his* advisedly because at this time there were no female animals in the Camel Corps) to beguile you into thinking he was as harmless as a babe. All the grace and charm of the brutes, however, were seen at their best when they were either getting up or lying down. The process of settling down began with unearthly guttural noises and screeches on the part of the riders, with anxious requests to *barrak** and a tugging at the rope attached to its mouth.

The procedure of the camels themselves never varied. At first they protested with many grunts and deep-throated noises, and jerked their heads back in angry remonstrance. Then they sank gradually on their knees and remained there until they had suitably voiced their opinion of the whole matter. Once they came to the conclusion that after all they might be more comfortably off lying on the sand than standing, they arranged their legs and finally sank on their stomachs with their limbs half buried in the sand. The reverse process was equally intricate: a long pause before the camels made up their minds, then a lurch backward, followed by a sudden lurch forward which made the rider long for the calm of a Bight passage.

The Cameliers were not long in finding out that the camels most delicate spot was the tender portion of its abdomen, and that a vigorous back-heeler from an army boot was always sufficient to set the brute's lifting machinery going at full speed.

The days passed in saddling, mounting, dismounting, feeding, and riding the camels over the sands of Abbassia, and on the historic ground where Camel Corps units had been trained in bygone years. At first we spent hours compelling the brutes to *barrak*; then we mounted them without saddles, and fell off again when they suddenly rose to their feet. By the time we were issued with saddles we had become expert at mounting

---

* Sink to their knees.

them in the way described. The saddles were wooden affairs with a hole in the top which fitted over the hump on the camel's back. One or more neatly-folded blankets placed in the bed of the saddle, and over the hump, provided us with a comfortable seat. Then we walked, trotted, and raced the animals from the training-ground to the sandy stretch of country that extended to the base of the age-worn Mokattam Hills.

As Captain Barber reluctantly admitted, these Australian infantry men took to camel work like a duck does to water. Soon we were issued with the full equipment that was to be our property so long as we remained in the Camel Corps. This consisted of rifle with two hundred and forty rounds of ammunition, and, on one side of the saddle, and held in position by leather straps which fitted over the front and rear of the saddle, a galvanized-iron *fantass* to hold five gallons of water. This weight was nicely balanced on the opposite side by a canvas bag, which held fifty pounds of *durra* — food for the animals when travelling long distances, or patrolling many miles from our base. A basil apron covered the upper part of the camel's neck to prevent friction by the rider's boots which rested on it. Head-stall and girth were of leather; the rein to guide the animal was of rope. Two canvas bags, attached by a strip of the same material, were thrown across the saddle covering the fantass and *durra* bag. These held our clothing, food, and the aforesaid ammunition. Months later, when it was difficult to procure firewood for cooking purposes, we carried what fuel we could find, borrow, or steal, on the back of the saddle; while cooking-utensils were attached to any part of the saddle that offered a place where they could be fastened.

One night two inebriated Cameliers staggered from the canteen at Abbassia, and probably seeking further excitement, saddled their camels and rode forth into the night. They had no idea where they were going, and didn't care. Next morning they were reported missing, and later the Gyppo attendants announced that two camels, with full equipment, had also disappeared. Mounted Cameliers raced in different directions. The missing men were found fast asleep on the sand, many miles beyond Heliopolis, with the loaded camels *barraked* beside them.

Paraded at headquarters, Captain Barber cast a swift glance of contempt at them.

"Call them British soldiers," he said scornfully. "Bah! Take them to the guard-room. They ought to be back in Australia throwing boomerangs at crows."

Although he was rarely seen on the parade-ground during the early training days of the new unit, Lieutenant-Colonel (afterwards Brigadier-General) C. L. Smith, V.C., M.C., who had been brought from England to command the newly-formed Camel Corps, watched their training with the keenest interest. This gallant soldier was awarded the coveted military decoration during a single-handed encounter with hostile natives in Somaliland. Firing the last cartridge out of his revolver he knocked out the only surviving native with his fist, then picking up a wounded officer, and a native medical orderly, one on each shoulder, he staggered back to the British lines.

Our G.O.C. had no illusions about the type of men he was to command. Their deeds on Gallipoli had convinced him they would be able to endure the hardships of desert campaigning over a wide area, and would give a good account of themselves in a tight corner. He realized that strict discipline was not to their liking, and to get the best out of them they had to be treated with a certain amount of leniency when paraded before him for some crime with which they had been charged. Still, there were times when these Cameliers did things that made him wonder if he would ever make good soldiers of them.

One morning the felt hats were taken from the men in the battalion, and pith helmets were issued instead. The Diggers resented this, and the same night many of them kicked the crowns out of their new headgear. The following morning scores of damaged helmets were scattered over the sands of Abbassia, and the Cameliers paraded bareheaded. That afternoon their felt hats were returned to them, but Lieutenant-Colonel Smith made no secret of the fact that he was annoyed.

A silent man at most times, I saw him laugh heartily on one occasion only. A brawl had taken place in one of the huts the previous night, and soon afterwards the G.O.C. was informed that one of the Cameliers had tried to set fire to another man sleeping in the same hut. This alarming report was greatly exaggerated; when the true facts were related to the G.O.C. he laughed until there were tears in his eyes.

It was customary to call the roll in the huts every night at 9.30. On this particular night a sergeant had returned from Cairo in a hilarious mood. Dressed only in boots and singlet, and carrying a roll-book in one hand and a lighted candle in the other he began his inspection of the huts. Entering the first hut he looked around for some place to put the candle while he called the roll. Sighting one of the men lying asleep on his back he tipped the candle, poured the hot grease on the sleeper's forehead, and stuck the candle upright in it.

With a wild yell the sleeper awoke; the next moment a sergeant, with a flimsy singlet fluttering in the wind, fled in the direction of the nearby Mokattam Hills closely pursued by another lightly-clad Camelier. The following morning both of them showed on their faces the marks of a fierce fistic encounter under a starlit Egyptian sky.

One morning, when we were engaged in mounted drill on the training-ground at Abbassia, two strange officers arrived on the scene. They keenly watched every movement of the Cameliers, then one of them turned to Lieutenant-Colonel Smith.

"How long have these men been training?"

"Two weeks."

"Wonderful. I've been training men in the Sudanese Camel Corps for years, and it would take them months to be as well-drilled and as skilful at handling camels as these Australians."

One morning No. 1 and No. 2 companies of the Camel

Corps turned their backs on the training-grounds of Abbassia and rode forth to the Great Adventure. There was a song on their lips, and their hearts were light. Some weeks later the remaining two companies followed them, and the Military Police in Cairo muttered, thank God, they're gone." Standing in front of the Camel Corps headquarters, Captain Barber watched their departure. There was a queer smile on his face: for many minutes he did not speak. Then he turned to Sergeant Bannister, the orderly room sergeant:

"By gad, they look as innocent as sucking babes, but God help the enemy that meets those fellows."

Chapter 2

When the Senussi, the most powerful native tribe in Egypt, began to listen to German agents at the latter end of 1915, and accept such bribes as English sovereigns, silks, musical instruments, and other things that appealed to the Arabs, the British prepared for trouble from a new quarter. It was not long in coming. One morning the Senussi hordes, yelling and waving firearms, galloped away from their desert stronghold, El Jarabub, and swooped down on the Dakhla and Kharga oases. For a time they did not meet with much opposition. Several villages, such as Sollum, and Mersa Matruh, on the shores of the Mediterranean, were garrisoned by small units of Egyptian and Sudanese soldiery, led by British officers, but they only put up a feeble resistance against the stronger forces of the Senussi.

A Western Frontier Force came into existence, and ere were several skirmishes, chiefly between the Senussi and British yeomanry units. Twenty miles to the west of Mersa Matruh, a regiment of yeomanry charged the Arabs, only to see the ranks of the enemy open in the centre, and the British mounted troops galloped headlong over a thirty-foot cliff, with the result that most of the men and horses were killed.

Realizing that more drastic methods would have to be adopted if the Senussi were to be suppressed, a powerful force was now sent to the western frontier. It consisted mainly of English yeomanry, Australian light horse, and half a flight of the Royal Flying Corps. They encountered the Senussi at Gebel Medwa, six miles south-west of Mersa Matruh, on Christmas Day, 1915, and after a fierce battle lasting until the following day, the enemy were routed, leaving two hundred of their dead lying where they fell.

Three weeks later one of our airmen noticed the Senussi congregating in large numbers at Halazin, and a strong force, consisting mainly of British yeomanry, Australian light horse, and South African infantry moved out from Mersa Matruh. A splendid body of men were the South Africans. From 3 a.m. to 10 p.m. they marched seventeen miles across wastes of yellowish white sand, and their feet became blistered and swollen. After resting for several hours the troops again moved forward, and covered eight miles before they came to where the Arabs were entrenched on a low sandy ridge. The Senussi were waiting for them. No doubt the movements of our men had been watched overnight by prowling Arabs, who then made their way ahead of the British to acquaint the enemy with the number of men who were advancing towards where they were entrenched. Several shells from a couple of nine-pounders burst over the British troops as they came in sight of the enemy trenches, then our lines were swept by machine-gun fire. Many men fell, but the remainder continued to advance in a series of short rushes. The South Africans were limping painfully; many of them removed their boots, then fought barefooted.

Towards evening the South Africans, yelling their war-cry charged the enemy trenches, and the Arabs fled in all directions, but not before hundreds of them were shot down. Once they started to run the British shot them as fast as they could press trigger. Soon the ground was dotted with the dead and dying. The British losses were twenty-eight killed and two hundred and seventy-four wounded, while the Senussi had six hundred and fifty killed and wounded.

The Senussi, reinforced by several hundred other tribesmen, soon afterwards took up a strong position at Agagiya. Again the South African infantry charged their trenches and routed them. At the same time the Dorset Yeomanry, led by Lieutenant-Colonel Souter, charged with drawn swords across a wide open valley towards where the Arabs had again entrenched themselves, and the fire from four machine-guns in their possession was responsible for many casualties amongst the charging horsemen. Then they began to fire wildly, and the bullets from their guns whistled over the heads of the Dorsets.

In front of his men galloped Lieutenant-Colonel Souter, and his courage earned the admiration of the Colonial troops who were witnessing a dashing cavalry charge for the first time. Nearing the Arab trenches his horse was shot from under him, and when he rose from the ground he found himself face to face with Jaafar Pasha, the Turkish leader of the Senussi fighting force, who immediately surrendered to him. Souter then raced ahead on foot, slashing his sword to left and right.

"For forty b------years I've been waiting for this," he cried.

Seventeen days later No. 2 Company of the Imperial Camel Corps, with other British troops, occupied Sollum, and the same day the Duke of Westminster with his armoured cars proceeded toward Bir Hakkim, a hundred and twenty miles to the west, where the crews of the armed steamer *Tara* and *S. S. Moorina* were held prisoners by the Senussi. Their ships had been sunk by a German submarine in the Bay of Sollum four months previously. Their treatment while in the hands of the Arabs was one of the most distressing incidents of the war. Forced to march with blistered feet over the scorching sands, they were imprisoned for many days in a filthy well, and were even compelled to eat snails. Four of the seamen died from ill-treatment, and the others resembled scarecrows when rescued by the Duke of Westminster's armoured cars. They cried like children when food was given to them by the Cameliers; many of them were so weak that they were sent to hospital after arriving at Sollum.

When the Senussi were less troublesome the mounted troops and infantry were withdrawn, and returned to the banks of the Suez Canal. Then the first four companies of the Imperial Camel Corps, supported by the Duke of Westminster's armoured cars, began to patrol the desert wastes from different centres. For six months we were engaged in patrolling operations from Luxor, four hundred miles south of Cairo, to Sollum, on the Mediterranean coast.

Although engaged in no fighting worth mentioning, the Cameliers kept the Senussi at a distance. Desert patrolling, however, was dreary work, and soon we were longing for something more active. To our inflamed senses the horizon seemed a prisoning ring of red-hot bronze. As far as sight could reach stretched sand— white monotonous wind-ribbed sand that lacerated mercilessly the eyes of man and beast. Though we generally carried six days' supply of drinking-water when on patrol duty, we had to be careful how we used it Patrols went away from their bases for days, and at last, with their tanks almost empty, drank the tepid liquid that was worse than the chlorinated water served out upon the shrapnel-torn beach at Anzac.

One company of Cameliers, operating from their base at Kharga, proceeded on a longer patrol than was intended when they rode out toward the open desert. On the sixth day they found themselves with little or no water in their tanks. Their plight was desperate. Two men, after swallowing what little water could be given them, volunteered to race their camels back to Kharga and have water sent out to them. They reached their destination half crazed with thirst and swaying in their saddles. Water-laden camels were hurriedly raced toward the stricken patrol, and out on a desert waste, where heat waves shimmered, they came on men with swollen tongues and scorched lips. Several of the Cameliers had to be sent to hospital in Cairo.

Another patrol, several days out from their base at Mersa Matruh, came to a native well, and eased their parched throats with the water they found in it. It had a peculiar taste. The water was bailed out of the narrow hole, and at the bottom lay a long-dead Arab. Fleeing on foot from the British troops, after a desert skirmish, and perhaps wounded, he had staggered to this well, weak and exhausted, and had toppled down it when he leaned over the top to reach the water below.

When the Cameliers first came to Mersa Matruh they found much to interest them during these desert patrols, Scattered about the desert were crumbling and half-buried ruins of long-dead cities that once stood beside the ancient caravan route between Alexandria and Carthage. At Mersa Matruh a few scattered stones marked the site where Cleopatra, the last queen of ancient Egypt, had a summer residence. The Cameliers were able to purchase tinned delicacies in a native store, and during the first few days they took a keen interest in an aged marquee used as a canteen, but where beer of a sort was sold.

Within a few hours after their arrival at this historic little village, on the shores of the Mediterranean, the Cameliers were informed their presence was not desired at the canteen. This was conducted for the benefit of an English mounted unit, and men connected with the Duke of Westminster's armoured cars. Some months previously, so the Tommies said, several tall and wiry light horsemen had caused a disturbance within its canvas walls. After that the Tommies decided the canteen, with its liquid contents, would be taboo to any troops from Australia.

The Cameliers were disappointed. They had money, and they also had a thirst that could only be satisfied with copious draughts of beer. They discussed the matter among themselves, and then Snowy Allen had a brilliant idea. He said the Tommies had informed him the Duke of Westminster was a sport, and that although he owned a big slice of London there was no swank about him. Snowy suggested he approach the duke, and plead for his permission to allow the Cameliers to patronize the canteen.

Back from a desert patrol, the duke, as he stepped from a dust-stained car, was confronted by a hard-faced, grinning Camelier. Saluting in a haphazard way Snowy wasted no time in explaining why he was there.

"Look here, look," he began, "we only lobbed here to-day,

and we can't get a drink at the canteen. It ain't fair. Just because a couple of wild and woolly light horsemen let their heads go here a couple of weeks back, we are not allowed to enter the place. I reckon—"

"What are you talking about, man, and who are you?" Said the Duke of Westminster, as he leaned against the side of the car.

"Me!" Replied Snowy. "Oh, my name's Allen, and I belong to the Camel Corps. We only rode in here this afternoon, and those fellows in charge of the canteen won't let us go inside the blanky place because we are Australians."

"Well, if you have any complaints to make, approach your officer, otherwise I can do nothing for you," said the duke, as he started off towards his tent.

"But look here, sir," said Snowy, following behind, "we ain't light horsemen. We're infantry men from Gallipoli, and we know how to behave ourselves anywhere. We ain't like those light horse fellows. They don't know how to behave themselves when there's beer about. If you will allow us into the canteen we'll prove to you that the Australians in the Camel Corps are gentlemen."

Just then Snowy realized that the Duke of Westminster had disappeared inside his tent, and that he was addressing a group of grinning English car mechanics, who had overheard most of the conversation. Muttering under his breath Snowy returned to where we were bivouacked.

Still, his interview with the duke was not in vain. Soon afterwards we were informed that the canteen would be open to men from the Camel Corps for two hours after tea, provided we "played the game." During the first hour the Cameliers and Tommies drank to each other's health, and after several drinks vowed that together they could wipe the desert with all the Senussi in Egypt. They even shook hands on it. One hour later someone started an argument. That led to blows. Soon several khaki-clad men were fighting, and just as the lights were extinguished inside the canteen, Snowy Allen was heaved outside by a burly English trooper.

That was the end of the canteen; it did not open again. When the Duke of Westminster's armoured cars departed toward Alexandria some days later they took it with them; only a stack of empty bottles lay on the sand to mark the spot where it once stood.

The Cameliers soon found other things to interest, and perhaps annoy them. The sand on which we slept, dined, and passed idle hours was infested with fleas. Tommy Hodgson said there were ten millions of them to a square yard of sand. We took his word for it and put up with them. If a handful of sand was lifted and allowed to trickle through the fingers a score of fleas would hop from it. Snowy Allen said they were big hairy fellows with a white spot on their backs, and that they bore a slight resemblance to the fleas that had worried us in the dugouts on the slopes of Anzac.

When the morning sun shed its fierce rays on the desert sands we spread our blankets in the open, and the fleas that were exposed to the heat hopped under them. We turned the blankets and again the fleas hopped under them. It was a great game—for the fleas. At last we took our blankets down to the beach and spread them on the wet sand. The insects did not like the wet sand, and we slumbered soundly without being disturbed.

One of the camel patrols returned to Mersa Matruh with the information that the Senussi had a fondness for English sovereigns, and always carried them in a leather belt pressed next to their bodies. That started us thinking. We all hoped to return to Cairo in the near future, and golden sovereigns would provide us with many things we desired in the city of the Caliphs. We remembered that in a gorge at Gebel Medwa there lay many dead Senussi who had not been buried when they were slain in battle the previous Christmas Day. Some of the Cameliers went out and searched the dead and decaying corpses. They came back with sovereigns.

One Camelier placed his easily-gained wealth in an empty pickle bottle, and scooping a hole in the sand inside his tent, during the absence of his tent mates, left it there. Emerging from the tent he was selected to accompany several other Cameliers moving out on a six days' patrol. There was no time to unearth the bottle of sovereigns and take it with him. Buried deep in the sand, and every man who occupied the tent accompanying him on the patrol, he was confident his hidden wealth would not be disturbed. As he rode over the desert sands, or lay at night near some shady oasis, he planned what he would do with those thirty sovereigns when he again returned to Cairo. There would be grilled steaks and lager beer at the St. James cafe, other meals at Groppi's, and perhaps there would be odd moments when he would be charmed by the smiles of "Tiger Lil" or Marcelle.

Weary and dust-covered the patrol returned to Mersa Matruh on the sixth day, to find that during their absence the tents had been moved half a mile along the beach. The ever-moving sands had hidden all trace of where the tent, with its hidden wealth, had formerly stood, but during the time the Cameliers were stationed at Mersa Matruh a worried Australian unsuccessfully dug up acres of sand, hoping to find the buried bottle with its golden contents.

One morning a patrol moved out from Mersa Matruh and travelled thirty miles inland to watch and report the movements of straggling bands of Senussi who were supposed to be making toward their main army. The patrol was in charge of a lieutenant, who was not popular with the men; he was one of those individuals who could be told nothing. When he reluctantly confessed he did not know where he was, none of the Cameliers offered to assist him to reach his destination.

Around the patrol, and extending as far as the eye could reach, was drab sand and patches of low scrub where timid quail concealed themselves as we approached. After riding in circles for several hours, and getting nowhere, the officer reluctantly turned to his men.

"Look here," he said, "some of you fellows have been prowling about this blasted desert longer than I have. Do any of you know where we are?"

Snowy Allen wheeled his camel and rode up beside the officer.

"Yes, sir," he said in a hoarse whisper, "something tells me we are on active service abroad."

Those who overheard the remark roared with laughter, but the officer, losing his temper, snapped back:

"Yes, Allen, and something tells me that if we get back to Mersa Matruh you will suffer for this impertinence."

Before the patrol did return to its base the officer had forgotten his grievance against Allen, and nothing more was heard of the incident.

A camel patrol was ordered to move out from Kharga to search for a lost British aeroplane. Days previously two observation planes flew away from Kharga to watch the movements of a band of Senussi. One of them developed engine trouble, and compelled Lieutenant Ridley, of the R.F.C., and Garside, his mechanic, to make a forced landing on a desert waste. The other plane also landed, and the pilot ordered the two men in the damaged machine to remain where they were until assistance arrived. Then the undamaged machine flew back to Kharga, and an Australian camel patrol rode out to the assistance of Ridley and his mechanic.

On the second day the patrol came to where the machine had rested for a time, but there were marks on the sand to show it had taken off again. The patrol went back to Kharga, but the missing airmen had not returned. Again the Cameliers faced the open desert, and searched for days over that naked and sinister waste beneath the high blue of the sky. Other planes flew backwards and forwards, hoping to see below them a small speck that on closer inspection would reveal itself as a damaged machine.

Seven days out from Kharga, and with their faces blistered by the fierce heat, the camel patrol halted. A keen-eyed sergeant had pulled up his camel with a jerk, and with a hand shading his eyes stared long at something white that lay on the sand ahead. He rode across and spoke to an officer. Then the camels, bubbling fretfully, were urged forward again, and soon the Cameliers came to the missing plane. Lying beside it were two dead men.

Scattered around were empty bully-beef tins and biscuits, but there was no water. Near the body of one man lay a diary that told the story of the forced landing, how the men had tried to fly back to their base only to be forced down again miles away from their starting-point. The last entry in the book read: "Lieutenant Ridley shot himself at ten o'clock on Sunday morning.... He was a gallant gentleman."

Soon after he wrote these lines, Garside, the mechanic, also passed away

Chapter 3

"I'd like to know what you and I are supposed to be doing in this God-forsaken part of the world," muttered Snowy Allen to his camel, as he picked ticks from the animal's hindquarters. "We've been wandering around this desert for the past six months, doing nothing in particular, yet we're supposed to be fighting for the Empire. There's me old dad, back on the Riverina, writing every mail to know when I'm going to win the V.C. Nice chance a man's got to win a decoration when there's no fighting going on. I'm fed up with it all, and I've a good mind to write to the War Office, and ask them if this is a war, or a blanky picnic. Yes, I'll------"

Just then the camel let out a side kick, and narrowly missed Snowy's head. Without looking back to see if there was a chance of getting in another kick with better success, the animal curled its bottom lip contemptuously and stared out across the desert.

"Well, of all the ungrateful, four-legged, stupid blanky animals that came out of the old ark you're the worst," cried Snowy, as he sat on the sand, where he had fallen in his haste to avoid the kick. "Here I've been as good as a father to you, and if I didn't keep picking the ticks from your ugly, stinking carcass they'd eat you alive. If it wasn't that I'd get a blob of red ink as big as the map of Egypt put into me pay-book for not doing me duty I'd let them eat you."

Ten minutes later Allen was in his tent listening to the latest news, "straight from the horse's mouth," as the sergeant put it. The Cameliers were to concentrate beside the Suez Canal, and then assist to chase the Turks back across Sinai. There was going to be some heavy fighting, and the Cameliers were to have their share of it.

"There you are," said Allen, addressing anyone who cared to listen to him, "I knew it was too good to last. We've been having a nice little holiday, but instead of allowing us to remain here someone has to interfere, and we've got to go into the firing-line again, where a fellow might get killed, or wounded, or taken prisoner. Turks compel prisoners to break stones on the roads up Aleppo way, and me delicate constitution would never stand that kind of work. Me old dad once said that------"

"Never mind about your dad," snapped back the sergeant. "Unless you're dashed lucky you'll never see him again. It's fellows like you who do foolish things in battle, then stop a lump of lead, and the next thing you know is that old Peter is issuing you with a rusted harp and a pair of mildewed wings."

"You're a funny fellow, you are," growled Allen. "I suppose when we get into our first scrap I'll be carrying you on me back while the disturbance lasts."

Here Allen glared at the sergeant for a few seconds, then walked out of the tent.

"Good man that," said the sergeant, looking at Allen's retreating figure. "If ever I've got to go into a tight corner he will be the first chap I'll pick to accompany me."

Although the Cameliers believed the report was only a *furphy*,★ on this occasion they were wrong. Three days later, with full equipment on their camels, they turned their backs on the shores of the Mediterranean, and rode toward Cairo.

During their absence on the western frontier the Camel Corps had greatly increased in strength. The first four companies had proved such a valuable asset that it was decided to add others to the Corps. At this time sufficient Australians were not available for the purpose, so the 2nd Battalion, consisting of No. 5, No. 6, No. 7, and No. 9 companies and later No. 8 and No. 10 companies was composed of English and Scottish Territorials, the former mostly transferred from the yeomanry units, and the latter from the Scottish Horse. Later, a third battalion, consist-

---

★ Camp rumour.

ing of No. 11, No. 12, and No. 14 companies, was formed from Australian Light Horse regiments, and No. 15 Company, which completed the battalion, consisted of reinforcements from the New Zealand Mounted Rifles. The force now became known as the Imperial Camel Corps.

At the latter end of 1916 a fourth battalion, consisting of No. 13, No. 17, and No. 18 companies, was formed from Australians recently arrived in Egypt. Many of these men had enlisted as Cameliers back in Australia, but a section of them had been transferred from what had previously been known as the Double Squadron. No. 16 Company, which completed this battalion, was formed from reinforcements for the New Zealand Mounted Rifles.

These eighteen companies, each with six officers and a hundred and sixty-nine other ranks, were supported by mobile artillery, provided by the Hong Kong and Singapore Battery, better known to the Cameliers as "The Bing Boys." There was a remarkable bond of friendship between the Indians in the battery and the men in the Camel battalions. These sturdy and well-trained Sikhs and Mohammedans were mostly ex-Indian Army regulars, and on many occasions they displayed such reckless bravery when under enemy shell-fire that they soon earned the admiration of the Cameliers. They accompanied the Camel Corps from the Canal until the unit was disbanded, and formed into light horse regiments.

The full fighting strength of the Hong Kong and Singapore Battery, attached to the Imperial Camel Corps, consisted of two hundred and forty Indians, with six British and four Indian officers. They carried on camels six mountain guns which fired nine-pounder shells.

A mobile veterinary section consisting of a hundred and forty Egyptians under a British officer, also accompanied the Camel Corps on their advance from the Suez Canal to Palestine. There were also several Sudanese regulars who were mainly responsible for the erection and working of the field-telephone service. These Sudanese were splendid types of manhood, and showed themselves fearless under fire. Somewhat reserved they kept a good deal to themselves, and were not so familiar with the Cameliers as were the Indians and Egyptians.

Advancing toward Palestine the Camel Corps Field Ambulance kept within easy distance of the different battalions, and treated many of the casualties in our ranks after the different battles in the Holy Land.

War is a funny thing. Ask the soldier who has had his share of it. In the firing-line, with death hovering round most of the time, the average fighting man will give everything he possesses to be back at the rear where there is no killing or mangling of human flesh. Leave him at the rear for a few days and he will start complaining that things are tame, and wishing that something would happen to break the monotony. What he wants is to be mixed up in a real front-line disturbance, just for a few hours. Put him in the front line, and after the first "hop over," or mad dash across the open, he craves for the rear again, where there are no whining bullets or crashing shells.

That is why several of the Cameliers bivouacked in the vicinity of the Suez Canal during the latter part of 1916 began to complain about the dreary existence they were leading. It was nothing but patrols, day after day, out on the burning sands of Sinai. Over in France the Australians were fighting, and could write letters home to prove they were doing the job for which they had enlisted. In their letters from Egypt the Cameliers could write about sand, and camels, and Gyppos, but there was no fighting worth mentioning.

Some of the men received letters from home informing them they were lucky they were not in France. That hurt. Others were told they knew what they were doing when they joined a mounted unit that was having a glorious time with the bints (girls) in Cairo, or riding around the historic ruins in the land of the Pharaohs. The Cameliers crushed such letters in their hands and swore.

Trooper Morrissey, of the Camel Corps, made no secret of the fact that the camels would not see him much longer.

"I'm going to France, even if I have to swim there," he said to those who cared to listen. "One of these fine days I'll be missing, and when you hear from me again I'll be doing something. I didn't come over here to pick ticks off stinking camels, and ride over miles of sand on the slobbering brutes. I came over here to fight, and I'm going where there's fighting to be done." We did not take much notice of Morrissey. Most of the Cameliers had been talking like that during the past few months. Several of us had tried to persuade our officers to use their influence on our behalf so that we would be transferred to one of the infantry units in France. But each time we were told to go back to the lines, and not mention the matter again. We went back to the lines, and the camels, and the sunscorched sands.

One morning Morrissey paraded before the O.C., and was granted seven days' leave to Alexandria. The seven days passed, but he did not come back to the company. Weeks passed, and then he was posted as a deserter.

We had almost forgotten about Morrissey when he came back to us. He didn't say much. In Alexandria he had met several Australian infantry reinforcements proceeding to England. They assisted him to conceal himself on the transport, and two weeks later he was in England.

"I'm only there two days when one of the Military Police sticks me up and asks for my pass," he said, with a far-away look in his eyes. "When I couldn't produce it I was shoved in the clink, and then they sent me back to Egypt."

"And didn't you have to face a court martial when you got back to Cairo?" Asked big Mick Burke.

"They don't court-martial good soldiers," drawled Morrissey, as he turned his back on us, and strode over to the camel-lines to see if the animal he had previously ridden was still there.

Several days later we were surprised to hear Morrissey had been awarded the Meritorious Service Medal. We couldn't understand it, and Morrissey would say nothing. It was not until one of the Cameliers came back from Cairo, where he had a sister nursing in the 14th Australian General Hospital, that we heard why Morrissey had been awarded the medal. On the transport which had conveyed him back to Egypt there were several sick and wounded men. Late one night the transport was torpedoed and soon sank. Finding himself in the water, Morrissey, who was a powerful swimmer, assisted many of the invalids to reach floating wreckage. Then he went to the assistance of two nurses who were exhausted, and kept them afloat until a destroyer picked up the survivors. One of the nurses he had rescued, said on her arrival in Egypt that Morrissey had been mainly instrumental in saving the lives of over twenty men and women, who would have been drowned had he not come to their assistance.

After that there was no need for us to wonder why Morrissey had not faced a court martial on his return to Egypt.

Then the Turkish hordes moved over the sands of Sinai toward the Canal. They met with success at Katia and Oghratina, and tried to break down our defences between Romani and the sea. Beaten back they turned their attention to the other flank, and fought desperately to secure possession of the chain of hills dominating this region. They had performed a wonderful feat in bringing an army of nearly thirty thousand men across a vast desert where wells were few and far between, and their nearest rail head was a hundred and fifty miles away. With them they brought on sledges heavy guns up to eight inches in calibre; a remarkable undertaking considering the nature of the country over which they were dragged.

Mount Royston and Mount Meredith both changed hands at least once, then came the terrific two days' battle at Wellington Ridge; but at last the Turks were beaten back by our mounted troops. Then the Imperial Camel Corps, in long straggling lines, moved out from their bases, and patrolled the flanks day and night. From a distance some of them watched the fighting around Romani, and grumbled because they could not take an active part in it.

"By God," said Mick Burke, "it's tough to see our cobbers up against it over there, yet we are not allowed to go and help them."

"If I know anything about it," replied another Camelier, "we'll get all the fighting we want before many hours have passed. Most of those men fighting over there are fagged out, and their horses want water. When they go back to rest we'll come into the limelight."

His words were prophetic. No. 4, No. 6, No. 9, and No. 10 companies, commanded by Major de Knoop (an Imperial regular officer previous to joining the Camel Corps) assembled at Barda, and were used in an effort to take the attention of the Turks in this sector away from the larger body of British troops opposed to them.

Soon afterwards these four companies, with two Australian Light Horse regiments under Lieutenant-Colonel C. L. Smith, V.C., Commander of the 1st Imperial Camel Corps Brigade, moved toward Mageibra, and at Aweidia, a short distance away, the English and Scottish sections of the corps were riding slowly over the sands, carpeted with short shrubbery, when they came on a party of Turks cleverly concealed. A machine-gun barked on the right, and a Tommy threw up his arms as a bullet struck him in the chest. With a soft gushing cough he lurched forward in the saddle, then toppled sideways and fell to the ground. His camel still plodded on.

"Here's where we are going to be forcibly reminded there's a war on," said Mick Burke to the sergeant riding beside him.

"Keep quiet," snapped back the officer riding a few yards in front. "You're here to fight, not talk."

"All right, all right," mumbled Burke. "But take it from me I'll be doing my bit when the whips start cracking."

Burke still mumbled, but no one took any notice of him. The eyes of every man were fixed on those bushes ahead, and they endeavoured to locate the spot where the machine-gun was concealed. It was still pouring forth a stream of lead, and the bullets were cutting up the sand all round the Cameliers.

Suddenly someone gave an order to dismount and lead the camels back to the rear. Then the men moved forward on foot. It was the first time under fire for many of them, but they soon became accustomed to the whine of bullets; and the necessity of taking advantage of every bit of cover that was available had been impressed upon them.

The Cameliers crouched, then dropped behind any rise of sand that lay in front of them. Here they fired several rounds from their tightly-gripped rifles, then dashed on again to another rise or clump of shrubbery.

In front, and not considering for one moment the danger ahead of him, Major de Knoop was setting a fine example to his men. "With bullets whining around him he motioned them to follow, and dashed forward. He had only proceeded a few yards when he fell, shot through the stomach. Ten minutes later he was dead.

"They shot him like a dog," cried a sturdy Tommy, as he raced toward the shrubbery where the Turks were concealed. He did not go far. A keen-eyed Turk took sight, pressed the trigger, and the Camelier spun on his heel, then fell forward on his face. The bullet had gone through his heart.

With the odds against them the Cameliers ceased rushing, and now took what shelter the low sandhills and shrubbery offered. Later in the day the 11th Light Horse Regiment engaged the Turks while the Cameliers slowly retired to where they had left their camels. Mounting they rode away from the scene of their first encounter with the enemy, and few of them spoke. Those in the English and Scottish companies were stunned at the loss of Major de Knoop, who had endeared himself to them by his gallantry, and attention to their welfare since he had taken charge of the four companies.

Captain G. F. Langley, who had served with the Australian infantry at Gallipoli previous to taking charge of No. 4 Company, now took over the command of the four companies, but he did not receive his promotion as major until several weeks had passed.

Chapter 4

Darkness had long since fallen when the Cameliers halted at Bir el Bayud after their silent ride from Aweidia. Without eating anything, most of us were soon asleep. It was still dark when we staggered to our feet. Officers were shouting commands, and men were hurrying in all directions. We rubbed our eyes and wondered what had happened. Then came the rat-tat-tat of machine-guns. Certain the Turks were charging us, we hurriedly picked up bandoliers and rifles, then stretched out behind any shelter that presented itself.

Funny things happen when men are fighting each other in open country. During the night, while we rode toward Bir el Bayud, the Turks, not aware of our destination, had also decided to bivouac at the same place, so as to water their horses at the wells next morning.

At dawn light horsemen noticed the enemy entrenched only a few hundred yards away. At almost the same time the Cameliers observed them, and Gunners Newport and Hazlett, of No. 4 Company, opened fire on them with Lewis guns. The rest of us sheltered behind a low sand-dune and began to pour a heavy rifle-fire toward the enemy trenches. Taken by surprise the Turks made only a feeble attempt to defend themselves, then began to retire.

Once again the Cameliers rode ahead, mostly on the wings. We were responsible for much of the patrol work carried out by our mounted units at that time. Day after day we rode with occasional short halts under a pitiless sky. It was 126 degrees in the shade, and there was no shade worth mentioning.

"You know, a fellow has his ups and downs in this world," said Mick Burke, as he edged his camel close to the animal I was riding, and growled about the broiling sun.

"Meaning when you get on and off a camel?"

"No. Back in Queensland I was a horse-breaker, and I could ride any buckjumper that was ever foaled in the Gulf country. I rode Bobs and Dargan's Grey, and all them noted horses that bucked their way around the State. Then I came over here, and just because I had a bit of an argument with the Military Police in Cairo I was transferred to the Camel Corps. If those old mates of mine back in Queensland were to see me now perched on the back of one of these stinking, blubbering brutes they wouldn't recognize me."

"Never mind, Mick, you're doing your bit; and that's all that matters just now," I said.

"Yes," he drawled, "but I'd sooner be doing it on the back of a horse. What's the good of these camels in a fight? You can't charge the enemy on them. Look what happened at Aweidia. That little stunt proved we could not disconnect from an engagement like horsemen. Why, if it hadn't been for those fellows in the 11th Light Horse most of us would now be playing Jews' harps in heaven."

A camel stumbled in front of us, and our conversation ceased. Still, it was good to talk on those long desert rides took our thoughts away from other things as it were; and there were things going on around us it was better to try and forget.

There was a constant shortage of water. The desert country over which we patrolled was a hundred miles wide, and there were few wells. Those we did come across contained brackish water we could not drink. Somehow the Turks managed to swallow it. At first our camels refused to drink it, but, when there was no other water available, they had to swallow it or die of thirst.

"A fellow would want a cast-iron stomach to hold that stuff," growled Burke. "Back in Australia I've drunk water that had dead cattle floating about in it. Used to boil it, then shut my eyes and swallow it. Boiling would make no difference with the fluid that's in these wells. Gripes, I'd like to have a front seat in a brewery just now."

"Don't worry, Mick. Ahead of us lies Palestine with its grape-fields and wine distilleries. You'll be set when you get there."

"Lead me to that glorious land," said Burke, as he dug the heel of his boot into the ribs of his camel and rode ahead. Soon he was chatting to Sergeant Williams.

"Hey, sarge," he began, "do you believe in spiritualism?"

"What makes you ask that question?" Replied Williams, who was well aware that Burke was one of the Hardest doers in the Camel Corps.

"Well, if you are one of those fellows who believes in spooks," went on Burke, "I'd like to know if there's half-way pub between Sinai and heaven?"

"How the blazes would I know," snapped back Williams. "I haven't been there to find out."

Mick grinned. "No. But if you don't keep your eyes open and your head down you'll blanky soon be there."

Sergeant Williams was a fine type of Australian soldier. He had brought a D.C.M. back from Gallipoli, and every man in his company knew he would give a good account of himself in a tight corner. Those are the sort of men soldiers like to have leading them when there's fighting to be done.

The light horsemen had a skirmish with the Turks at Mazar, but the Cameliers were well out on the right flank where we rode all night. A vast and gloomy silence seemed to press down upon us. We could see nothing before or around us, but we rode over one sand hill, then came to another, and rode over it. Those sandhills seemed to be unending. We would scramble up one side of them, then with gurgling snorts our camels would stop, and some of them plumped deliberately upon the sand. With low curses, and their boots beating a tattoo on the animals' ribs, the men urged them forward. It was a nightmare ride that lingered long in the memory of the men who took part in it.

Somewhere on the right the Bing Boys were experiencing similar trouble, but at last they dispatched a message stating they had lost connection with the main body. The message passed from mouth to mouth, and like many similar messages during wartime it was considerably altered when it was repeated to Captain Langley.

"Pass the word along to Captain Langley that the mountain battery has lost an axle," was the wording of the message when it was delivered to the officer Commanding the Cameliers.

A soft spoken and silent man at most times, Captain Langley swore when he heard this message. Had he not enough to think about in this wilderness of sand without the Indians worrying him about such an insignificant thing as a lost gun-axle. Might just as well try to find a needle in a haystack. He muttered under his breath and rode ahead. During the early morning hours the Bing Boys again linked up with us, and their white teeth showed in wide grins when we told them how their message had reached its destination.

Soon after this we rode toward Maghara, fifty miles south-east of Romani. Ahead of us rode Lieutenant P. Goldenstedt as guide. A Gallipoli veteran, he won his first commission at Lone Pine, and after the evacuation he transferred to the Camel Corps. He was the first adjutant to the 1st Camel Brigade formed on the field at Bir el Bayud, and he soon displayed to the Cameliers he did not know what fear meant. It was not long before he earned the reputation of being one of the best reconnaissance men in Sinai. Possessed of that casualness so characteristic of the Australian soldier, Goldenstedt liked nothing better than to be mixed up in a scrap with the enemy, and that was probably why he soon became one of the most popular officers in the Imperial Camel Corps.

Dawn was breaking when the Cameliers drew close Maghara, and they were reminded they were in the danger zone when they were fired on by a Turkish outpost. The light horsemen charged the main enemy position, and when close to it dismounted, then went forward on foot. The Cameliers had also left their animals in the rear, and with short rushes charged toward the trenches that held the enemy.

Ahead of them raced Lieutenant Paul Woods, with a service revolver in one hand and a Gurkha's kukri stuck in one of his putties. When eighteen hundred yards from the Turkish trenches he calmly proceeded to fire at any of the enemy who showed themselves. As the Turks were somewhat excited they often did this, and later Woods declared that, despite the distance between, he shot several of them.

"By cripes," whispered Burke, as we both rushed forward and threw ourselves down behind a sandy rise, where we watched Woods standing out in the open, loading his revolver while the Turkish bullets chopped the ground around him, "if Woodsie can shoot Turks at that distance I'd like to know how far he would have to be away from them to lop their heads off with that kukri stuck in his putty."

A bullet struck the sand in front of me, and when I had rubbed particles of it out of my eyes, I snapped back: "You'll get your fat head lopped off with a lump of flying ironmongery if you don't stop talking."

Burke grinned. "Getting windy?" And he fired at a head that showed itself for a second in front of him.

I did not reply. I was watching Lieutenant Woods away out in front, and expected to see him fall any minute. I wanted to see him reach that trench in front, and get busy with the keen-edged Gurkha knife he had now removed from his putty and was holding in his left hand while he still blazed away with his revolver.

I had watched Gurkhas using those knives when we fought for days and nights in the vicinity of Suvla Bay, and I knew what the weapons could do when handled by an expert. The headless Turks scattered Chocolate Hill, to the left of Anzac, were mute around evidence of the deadly work for which the little Indian hillmen had been responsible at close quarters

We got the order to retire, and Lieutenant Woods came back to us with his revolver and *kukri*. We did not see him in action again, as some weeks later he went to France.

After this the different Camel companies became scattered; those that went forward were detailed for patrol duty. Other companies came from the western frontier, and Abbassia when they had completed their training.

No. 3 Company, after patrolling the desert in western Egypt for several months, now arrived at Kantara, and rode toward Mazar. No history of the Imperial Camel Corps would be complete unless mention was made of this heroic unit. For many months before coming to Sinai a spirit of discontent existed amongst the men. It is difficult for me to express myself as I would like to do, and to set down here the real reasons for this discontent. The majority of the men had fought with the 1st Division at Anzac, and there they had proved themselves good soldiers. To put it bluntly, No. 3 Company was unfortunate in its leadership almost from the beginning.

Captain Fred Naylor, who took charge of the company when it proceeded from Abbassia to Mersa Matruh, was a fine soldier, and proved it when he was killed leading his men into action at Gaza. But he was a strict disciplinarian, and it was this characteristic which caused the men in his company to become so discontented that they lost no opportunity of transferring to other Camel companies. The remarkable thing about this officer is that, when he was with an infantry battalion before proceeding to Gallipoli, the men in his unit were greatly attached to him. With his own money he purchased articles of food not issued to them as army rations; gave them money when proceeding on leave; and chummed up with them at all times.

I am inclined to think those strenuous weeks at Anzac were responsible for Captain Naylor's changed attitude toward the men under him in the Camel Corps. I do know that when he was in No. 3 Company he suffered from ill-health. Malaria contracted in New Guinea prior to the war greatly troubled him. Perhaps he should have been invalided back to Australia after the evacuation.

The discontent which had been seething for many months in

this company came to a climax soon after the unit turned their backs on the Suez Canal. Slowly they rode onward over one of the most historic routes in the world—the great caravan track from Egypt to Palestine. The Cameliers were riding over a part of Sinai where Phoenicians, Romans, Jews, and Moslems had traded and fought. Napoleon came this way in his hurried dash into Egypt; and here, too, most of his army left their scattered bones. This highway was also hallowed by the journey of Joseph and Mary with the Infant Christ, fleeing into Egypt from the wrath of Herod.

After leaving Kantara, No. 3 Company came to where several English and Scottish units were bivouacked. Seeing a canteen where provisions could be purchased, the men expected Captain Naylor to halt so that they could fill their ration bags with tinned fruit, biscuits, or cigarettes. Captain Naylor did not give the order to halt, and muttering to each other the men rode onward.

Soon afterwards Captain Naylor left the company in charge of the second in command, but before his departure he issued instructions that we were to halt some miles ahead and await his return. Finding a suitable spot a short distance ahead the second in command save the order to halt. When Captain Naylor returned the men were about to have their meal. He wanted to know why they had not proceeded the distance he had instructed, and when the second in command offered his explanation he immediately ordered the company to continue their journey without eating the meal they had prepared.

The men counted him out, and after proceeding a few hundred yards, Captain Naylor rode back and warned them they would face a court martial if they persisted in their conduct. Again he was counted out, and by way of punishing the men he ordered them to dismount and lead their camels over the heavy desert sand. The Cameliers refused to walk and rode ahead. At one stage the situation looked ugly. Nearly every man carried his rifle pointed across his knee toward Captain Naylor.

Bivouacked at Mazar the men were congratulating themselves that Captain Naylor had forgotten the incident. But one morning several of them faced a court martial. The punishment meted out to them was that they rejoin their former units in France. Soon afterwards they left Sinai, and in their first engagement in France several of them were killed.

Chapter 5

A rooster crowed as we ended our long night ride from Mazar, and before us lay the desert village of El Arish.

That was the first rooster some of the Cameliers had heard since they left the shores of their native land; to them it revived memories of the days before Mars sounded his war-gong, and brought half the world into conflict against each other.

Snowy Allen voiced the feelings of many: "Spare me days! I'd kiss that bird if I could catch him, and then I'd take him with me as a mascot."

"Yes," drawled the man riding beside him, "and some day when bully-beef got on your nerves you'd turn him into stew."

"Not on your life. I'm as rough as bags, and as tough as nails; but, by cripes, the crowing of that old fowl touches a soft spot in my heart. Takes me back to the dad's farm on the Riverina, and------"

"Never mind about your dad's farm," interrupted Private Hegarty, who had overheard Allen's remarks about the rooster. "I'm not feeling too well at present, and if I have to listen to your chatter I might get homesick."

"Poor little fellow! Better see the M.O. when we get into camp and ask him for a couple of number nines."

"It's mag artists like you who make war what it is," growled Hegarty. "For the love of Mike, give that tongue of yours a rest, and then every man in this company will rejoice."

Allen was about to hurl a stinging retort when the order came to halt and dismount. Soon the Cameliers were sitting or lying on the sand, thankful for the opportunity of having a few minutes' rest after the long hours in the saddle.

There are Cameliers who will never forget that night ride toward El Arish. Leaving Mazar we rode over twenty-three miles of barren desert, and during the long ride little was heard except the curious bubbling noise made by the camels. Smoking was not allowed. As the night wore on men dozed in their saddles, then straightened themselves with a jerk as a whispered order came to halt. Then on again, wondering what was before us, and believing that the Turks would put up a stiff resistance at El Arish.

Dawn was breaking when we came across the first infantry-man we had met, lying on the desert sand. As we approached he raised himself on an elbow and pointing toward his mouth:

"Water!" He muttered.

One of the Cameliers pulled up his mount and filled the man's mess-tin with water from the fantass at the side of his saddle, and which held six days' supply —so precious in this barren country where wells were few and far between. Over the next sand-ridge we came on many more men, mostly belonging to a Scottish infantry unit. They also wanted water. Most of them had discarded their boots and nursed aching and swollen feet. During their long march they had drunk more of their meagre supply of water than was advisable, and toward morning were tortured by the pangs of thirst. The loose, coarse sand had worked its way into their boots, and so irritated the flesh that they began to limp, and eventually had to fall out from the ranks and remain behind. Their more fortunate comrades could not wait for them. Their objective was El Arish, to be attacked by foot and mounted units at dawn.

Many of these men gathered round one Camelier and appealed loudly for water, which was given to them until a Camel Corps officer issued a sharp command that no more water was to be given away.

"We do not know when we will get any more ourselves," he said.

It was hard to ride away leaving many thirsty Scotties behind, but orders had to be obeyed. "We knew the officer spoke the truth. Several days might pass before we came to some well where we could refill our fantasses. Some of us had gone without water during long patrols in the Libyan Desert: we did not want that experience again.

What attracted the attention of the Cameliers more than anything else as we approached El Arish was a large grove of date-palms. Beyond it the white roofs of a mosque and mud-constructed houses shimmered in the rising sun. It was good to gaze upon those palms after riding for weeks across desert sand, with no vegetation except a stunted bush here and there. We felt we would like to erect our bivvies under those palms, and for a time forget that there was such a thing as war.

Snowy Allen, as usual, spoke first. "I don't see why you fellows should be surprised at palms growing here." (He had left his camel to take care of itself, and joined a group of us squatted on our heels at the foot of the last sand-ridge overlooking the village.) "Didn't that padre bloke tell us back at Mazar that it was here the ancient river of Egypt once flowed until some sort of earthquake, or other violent disturbance caused it to disappear. The Arabs reckon the river now flows underneath, and I suppose that's why the surroundings are so fertile."

"Well, if I knew where it flowed I'd dig down and get sufficient water for a wash," said Private Baker. "I'm as dirty and lousy as any man between here and Cairo."

Lieutenant Rae, who was standing close by, grinned. "You haven't got that all on your own. There's chats playing hide and seek from my head down to my toes."

"Now, what do you think of that," Allen commented, as he gazed in astonishment at the speaker.

"What's wrong?"

"I never thought chats troubled officers. I always had an idea that the Almighty placed them on this earth to torment privates and lance-corporals."

"Well, they'll continue to torment you. You'll remain a private until the end of the war—unless Abdul collects you."

Just then we got the order to mount again, and soon were riding on the outskirts of the village. We had expected the Turks to make a stand here. During the two years they had occupied the village the enemy made elaborate preparations to hold it if attacked by the British. Its strategic position, and its value as a sea-port meant much to them. Yet for some unknown reason, the German staff decided at the last moment to evacuate the place. At Magdhaba, however, some twenty miles down the Wady El Arish, they left a strong force to delay our advance.

We halted and camped among the palms on the banks of the wady. Some of the men strolled around the village, and conversed in broken Arabic with the Bedouin inhabitants, who greeted the Cameliers with much enthusiasm. They would have greeted the Turks in the same way if they had returned the following morning.

We were about to erect bivvies and rest when the Cameliers, with the exception of No. 3 Company, received orders to saddle their tired mounts and ride toward Magdhaba.

With much grumbling the Cameliers prepared for another long night ride. Already the Light Horse and Royal Horse Artillery were moving out in long, straggling lines, and soon the Cameliers followed them. Knowing there was no water between El Arish and Magdhaba the Turks felt confident they would not be attacked for some considerable time. They did not think for a moment that mounted men, after riding all night, would again push forward on tired horses and camels and attack them at dawn.

Yet that is what happened. It was one of the most extraordinary exploits of the mounted men during the long months of desert campaigning on that front. It was the first time since the formation of the Imperial Camel Corps that they went into action with almost full strength. On this occasion they consisted of the 1st Battalion, in charge of Captain G. F. Langley, the 2nd Battalion under Major J. R. Bassett, and the 3rd Battalion in charge of Captain C. R. V. Wright. The Bing Boys also accompanied us with their mountain guns. We had now become so attached to the swarthy-faced, smiling Indians that the Cameliers would have complained if they took part in any engagement without these men, so skilled in the use of their light field-pieces.

As we moved out from El Arish the Bing Boys rode close to us, and with a gleam of white teeth one bearded Indian pulled up for a moment beside No. 1 Company.

"We're coming too, Johnnie," he said with a grin.

"By cripes, you'd better come, or there'll be something do-ing," replied a long lean Camelier.

The Bing Boys laughed. To them we were all "Johnnie" and they had no desire to know us individually by any other name.

It was a weary ride along the dry bed of the Wady El Arish. We were too tired to speak, and once again were not allowed to smoke. A few puffs at a cigarette would have cheered many of us, and helped us to forget that over forty hours had passed since we slept. There were times when we rode around in circles; stopped for short intervals; then rode on again in circles.

Day was breaking when we came in sight of Magdhaba. Soon afterwards we halted and barraked our camels near a Scottish battery. From there we had a splendid view of the light horse galloping forward and dismounting on our left. Then the 6th Light Horse came within range of the Turkish guns, and several shells burst above them. We expected to see many of them fall from their saddles, but they galloped out of the danger zone without any casualties.

The Cameliers received the order to advance, and in a long line we moved forward quite casually. We welcomed the order. After another all-night ride our legs and arms were stiff, and we felt sure that a brisk walk, with a certain amount of danger thrown in, would cause us to forget that we had not slept for many hours. Just as we moved forward the 2nd Light Horse gal-loped on the scene, dismounted, and leaving their horses behind linked up with our line on the right. Now we came within range of enemy rifle-fire. Although bullets tore up the ground around us they did not hit anyone; a leaden pellet smashed the stock of one man's rifle, but he still went forward carrying it with him.

Suddenly came the sharp command to lie down, and we threw ourselves full length on the sand. Here we lay for several hours with bullets whining around us and shrapnel bursting overhead. We did not mind the rest, as it gave many of us an opportunity to enjoy the first smoke since leaving El Arish.

Behind us the Bing Boys rode up on their camels, dismounted, and put their guns together. It was not long before they found the range, and their shells burst in rapid succession over the enemy redoubts. The Royal Horse Artillery were also getting in some good work, with the result that the Turkish gunners were firing wildly, and their shells were doing very little damage.

At such a time, with nerves highly strung, little things amused us. A private in No. 4 Company kept putting on and removing his helmet.

"What's wrong with you?" Asked the Camelier lying next to him.

"There's a sniper over there," was the reply. The man pointed to a rise some distance to the left of where we were lying. "He can see the white top of my helmet. About a million of his bullets have whizzed past my ears. I removed the dashed thing. Then I thought: if he fires at the helmet now he will miss it and hit me. So I put it on again. I've been doing that for the last quarter of an hour; and if we don't move soon he'll skittle me as sure as I'm lying here."

Stretched out on the sand we watched our airmen soaring over the enemy redoubts, and dropping bombs into their trenches. The Cameliers in the centre of the line were now in a perilous position. Without any cover to protect them they presented a fine target to the enemy gunners and riflemen. Their plight was desperate when the 3rd Light Horse dismounted and came to their assistance. Almost at the same time the Bing

Boys swept the Turkish trenches in front with their guns and somewhat diminished the fire of the keen-eyed Turkish riflemen.

With a muttered oath Mick Burke, lying beside me, ducked his head until his face was pressed in the sand.

"Nearly got you?" I asked.

"You bet it did," grinned Mick, raising his head a few inches. "Do you know that blanky bullet went so close to my head that I could hear the blessed angels whispering."

Then came an order for our company to advance toward a redoubt on the right, but before reaching it we had to cross a gully. We worked our way slowly down the sloping banks, and coming up on the other side our Lewis guns put up a sort of barrage. Then we rushed the enemy position with fixed bayonets. To our surprise several of the Turks jumped from their trenches to shake hands with us. Some who put up a feeble resistance fell at the point of the bayonet. Others would have met a similar fate had they not hoisted white flags.

Paddy Doyle, of No. 4 Company, rushed forward to take a rifle from a Turk, and caught it by the barrel, forgetting for the moment that the end of their rifles were devoid of woodwork. The rifle-barrel was red hot and Paddy's hand was badly burned. With anger blazing from his eyes he raised his rifle to bayonet the now terrified Turk, who was apparently appealing in his own language for mercy, but before he could do so he was stopped by another Camelier. Soon afterwards Doyle calmed down, and patted the Turk on the shoulder.

Walking up and down the trench Mick Burke was looking for cigarettes. Noticing one Turk with bulging pockets he dived his hand in without the Turk resisting, and pulled out a pouch of tobacco, also cigarette papers. As he did so a small bright object fell to the ground. Mick stooped and picked it up.

"Hullo, a Turkish Gallipoli Cross!"

The Turk nodded. He could not speak English, but he knew Burke recognized the decoration. "Put it there, old chap," said

Mick, holding out his hand which was immediately gripped by the Turk. "I was there myself, and it was such a hell of a place that you have my sympathy. Have a smoke!"

Here Burke handed him sufficient tobacco from the pouch to make a cigarette, then making one himself he put the rest of the tobacco in one of his tunic pockets.

"Give the poor cow his medal," said Tommy Hodgson. "They hunted us off the damned Peninsula, and he's entitled to it."

"Entitled to my fat aunt," sneered Burke, with a grin on his freckled face. "They didn't hunt us. We left of our own accord, nice and peaceful like. None of these officers about here will recognize my bravery, so I 'm going to decorate myself. Behold, before you stands Private Michael Burke, G.C."

Pinning the medal on his tunic Mick strutted along the trench, then came the order to charge another redoubt ahead. With a yell he hopped out of the trench and dashed ahead, a cigarette still in his mouth, and the medal on his chest.

Just about this time Lieutenant Williams, D.C.M., of No 4 Company, was badly wounded. Soon afterwards he was invalided back to Australia. He had received his commission at Abbassia, after the Katia operations, and was very popular with the men of his unit Another man in the same company who was wounded was Private Hopkinson, batman for Captain W P Cashman. Leaving the led camels he followed No. 4 Company's charge to the trenches with a camera in his hand. A keen photographer, he wanted a snap of the Turks surrendering. He got it; but he also got a bullet in the thigh, and did not rejoin his unit for several months.

During the remainder of the day trenches fell in rapid succession and there was not one company of the Cameliers that did not distinguish itself. Australians, Englishmen, Scotchmen, New Zealanders, and the Bing Boys firmly established the reputation of the Imperial Camel Corps as a fighting force. At the last wild rush our troops, in one wide encircling movement, surrounded the enemy who still resisted, and soon Magdhaba was in our hands. The Camel Corps casualties were remarkably light, considering the desperate fighting in which the men had participated.

Once again we turned our camels' heads towards El Arish. For the third night in succession we went without sleep. It was a ghostly army that straggled across sandy plains and down steep gullies. Not a man spoke. Many of them dozed in their saddles, awoke with a start when the column halted, then dozed again. To the right of us an Indian crooned a plaintive song as he rode along, and a man cursed when his camel tumbled. We were completely fagged out. Most of us would have given a month's pay to throw ourselves on the sand and go to sleep.

Somewhere along the line of Cameliers a sleepy voice broke the silence: "And it's Christmas Eve!"

No one answered him.

Chapter 6

"Men get queer in the head after they've been helping to keep a war going for several months," remarked Snowy Allen, as he dumped a wooden saddle on the back of his camel.

"I suppose you are referring to yourself?" drawled "Darkie" Fox.

"Well, yes. I'm satisfied I was not right in the head when I joined this blanky Camel Corps. These brutes are not fit for any respectable human being to handle. Blowing grubs a yard long out of their noses, and covered with ticks and mange. Ugh! I feel sick when I look at the stinking brutes."

"Yes, and the smell we get from associating with them sticks to a fellow when he goes on leave to Cairo," muttered Fox. "Remember when I went on leave last month? Well, in Cairo I meets a certain young lady called Fatima-el-Leile, otherwise 'Star of the night.' As soon as I goes up to her she tosses her head and holds her nose. 'A Camel Corps man,' she says. 'Poof! How you do smell! Pleese go an' have ze wash.'"

I bet that hurt. But who is this Fatima-el-Leile? I never heard of her."

"What! Never heard of 'Tiger Lil' Oh, go away and lose yourself."

Here Darkie Fox strolled away in the direction of the cook-house, and soon afterwards Snowy Allen was one of a patrol riding out from El Arish.

Some of the camels in the corps certainly took understanding. Out on patrols they often got a sudden idea into their heads not to go one step farther on their journey. At such times nothing would shift them. With a gurgling snort they would plump down deliberately on the sand and stay there. At first the Cameliers flogged them, but it was wasted effort. The camels refused to move. Then lighted matches were placed against certain tender portions of their bodies. They grunted, and remained where they were. One Camelier was so annoyed at his camel's stubborn behaviour that he gathered sticks, stacked them beside the animal's body, and placed a match to them. The flames sizzled the camel's hide, and soon there came the smell of burning flesh. The camel opened his mouth and gurgled, but did not move. In disgust the Camelier kicked away the burning sticks, then sat down to wait until the animal felt inclined to proceed on his way.

Most of us soon became accustomed to this eccentric behaviour, and when a camel "went on strike" while we were on a desert patrol, we did not waste words on him, but removed our blankets from the saddle, spread them on the sand, and went to sleep. Occasionally we awoke to find the camel a fast disappearing speck on the horizon; then there was a long walk ahead of us.

There were camels that went mad. One such brute "went wild" soon after we captured the last trench at Magdhaba, and proceeded to chase every man who came near him. At last the camel noticed an M.O. who had just finished attending to the wounded, and promptly chased him. The M.O. ducked and dodged in every direction, and sought shelter behind a stack of forage. The camel followed. Some of us were seriously thinking of shooting him when he stopped, and began to devour the durra behind which the doctor had taken refuge.

When we first became acquainted with camels at Abbassia, natives warned us to treat them with kindness, as they never forgot an injury. These men told the truth. One morning at El Arish, No. 15 Company bivouacked on a rise above where we had made our camp. Amongst them were several reinforcements recently arrived from New Zealand. A few hours after their arrival two of these men secured a long rope, and running in circles with it around one particularly bad-tempered camel they would suddenly jerk the rope and throw the animal to the ground. They did this several times. Then I went across and cautioned them to be careful of the brute if they went near him in future. The two New Zealanders ceased tormenting the animal, and probably soon forgot what I had told them.

The following morning one of these men was detailed to feed this camel. He had spread a bag on the ground in front of the animal, and was about to place durra on it when, with a snort of fury, the brute caught the man's arm in his mouth, whirled him in the air a couple of times, and finally threw him to the ground. The New Zealander's arm had to be amputated; he died, some days later, on his way to Cairo.

I had a narrow escape from being killed, or badly injured, by one of these mad camels. There was no doubt this particular animal was mad—in fact he was a "killer." No. 3 Company happened to have a slow Plodding animal that was no use to them, so they exchanged him for a fine, slim-limbed camel owned by some Arabs. Captain Naylor was quite pleased at the deal he had made. Soon afterwards, however, he learned that the brute was hopelessly insane. Tied to the lines day and night he would roar and foam at the mouth if anyone approached him. One day I was detailed to take the camels, on the lines, out grazing. Captain Naylor ordered me to take the mad brute with the mob. I mentioned that my life would be in danger if I did.

"You are here to do as you are told," said Captain Naylor. "If you do not obey orders you will be placed under arrest."

That settled it. Reluctantly I released the brute from the lines, and was surprised that he made no attempt to attack me or break away. He moved out with the other camels, and some time afterwards appeared to be grazing contentedly amongst them.

When out with camels on a grazing patch of country I generally dismounted on the outskirts of the mob, and, seated in the shade of some bush, would produce a writing-pad. I was busy over a page or two for the Sydney *Bulletin* when, looking up, I noticed that the mad camel had wandered from the other animals. For a few moments I thought his actions queer. Then it dawned on me that he was trying to persuade the other animals to follow him. Barraking my camel, I raced across on foot, and when only a few yards away from where he was standing I began to throw lumps of dirt at him. For a time he took no notice of me, then suddenly he threw himself on the ground, and began to foam at the mouth. Knowing what would follow I dashed away toward where the other camels were grazing, and, behind me, with long sweeping strides came the now infuriated brute. There were only a few feet between us when I reched the camels and dashed amongst them. The mad animal lost sight of me and commenced nibbling at the short grass.

Congratulating myself on my narrow escape from being pounded to death under the animal's chest, had he overtaken me, I went back to where I had left my saddled camel and once again took up my writing-pad. Half an hour passed, then I noticed that the mad camel was again becoming restless. A few minutes later he broke into a slow trot, and twice circled the bush near where I was seated. With loaded rifle in my hands I watched him, but at last he again returned to the mob, and I had no further trouble with him.

The following morning I again took the camels grazing; this time to a narrow gorge fringed on both sides by steep hills. There was another Camelier with me, and he stood guard at one end of the gorge while I remained at the other so that none of the animals could get away. Once again I had been ordered to include the mad camel with the mob. In the gorge he seemed to be restless. Twice he came within a few yards of where I was standing, but appeared to take no notice of me. Soon afterwards he trotted to the other end of the gorge and I felt sure he had forgotten about the incident of the previous day.

Seeing the animals were grazing contentedly I spread a blanket on the ground and stretched myself out to read an Australian newspaper that had arrived in the mail a few days before. An hour passed, then down the gorge came the sound of a galloping camel. It was the brute who had already caused me so much anxiety. This time he meant to get me. Coming closer he did not slacken pace, but with wide open eyes, and frothy foam flying from his mouth, dashed at me. I raised my rifle and fired, the bullet striking him in the centre of the forehead.

I expected to be placed under arrest when I reported to Captain Naylor that I had shot the camel. To my surprise he had little to say about the incident. Since then I have often thought that he was relieved at getting rid of a brute that would probably have killed someone had he remained with the company.

These camels certainly take understanding. I have known a Camelier, when ordered to rest during a night ride, use one of the animal's forelegs as a pillow. Barraking the camel down, he would place his head on the inside of the animal's nearside foreleg and lie there for, perhaps, two or three hours; but the leg would not be moved, although the camel would move the other three limbs from time to time, when he changed his position.

On similar occasions, when the camels were barraked, a blanket would be stretched from the top of one saddle to the other, then one or two men would crawl underneath it and go to sleep. I never knew the animals to move when men were sleeping like this between them.

Horses ridden by the light horsemen and yeomanry units could not, at first, be persuaded to go within a hundred yards of our camels; it took time to accustom them to the smell of the long-legged beasts. I remember a light horseman riding across to see his brother in No. 2 Company, also bivouacked at El Arish. While there a particularly angry camel stole up behind him. The light horseman heard the Cameliers' cries of warning, and looked over his shoulder. He had just time to stick spurs into his horse and gallop away. The camel followed him for a short distance, then plodded slowly back to the lines.

Arab stallions on issue to the Camel Transport Corps were different. Camels did not worry them. They stole the smellful animal's feed whenever they got the chance, and if an offending camel attempted to attack them they retaliated with several sickening double-footed hind kicks, right near where the camel stores his food. The majority of the camels were wary of these cheeky little horses, and always sheered away from them in that drifting way a camel has when scared.

One day word reached El Arish that a Scottish patrol, consisting of four men, had been attacked and killed by wild dogs in an isolated part of the desert. We didn't believe it. Then our own patrols, when they came back from long desert rides, told us about packs of famished dogs that followed them for miles. These animals, abandoned by Bedouins as they fled before the advance of the British troops, soon became daring. When two or three men went out with grazing camels the dogs would approach quite close to them once they dismounted, and had to be shot or they would have attacked the Cameliers.

There was a shortage of wood at El Arish, and we often rode miles before we could get sufficient to make a fire. The Cameliers saved the wooden portions of matches, and these, with dried camel-manure often gave us a chance to boil a dixie of water. One morning it was noticed that several poles belonging to an old telegraph line had disappeared during the night. They had been chopped close to the ground, and not even a splinter remained.

I was examining the short stumps that protruded from the ground, and had just finished hacking at them with a bayonet when two English yeomanry officers rode up. They also noticed that the poles had disappeared.

"Ha," said one of them, as he rode away, "the bally Australians have passed this way."

Certain light horse regiments had a fine supply of firewood during the days that followed, but the Cameliers continued to make fires with the assistance of wooden matches and camel-manure.

Chapter 7

Idle days followed for the Cameliers after their return from Magdhaba. Every morning small parties rode out from El Arish and returned late in the afternoon without meeting any of the enemy. Most of the time they kept a watchful eye on prowling Bedouins, who were suspected of spying on the movements of our troops.

These nomads of the desert, clad in filthy garments, showed their contempt for the Cameliers by refusing to answer questions, and chattering to each other in Arabic when we spoke to them. There were men in those patrols who would not have hesitated to put a bullet through one of them. But when an enraged Camelier threatened to use his rifle the officer in charge of the patrol generally managed to pacify him. Reluctantly we rode away from their encampments, storming inwardly as we saw the grins on their dusky and crafty faces. As soon as we disappeared from the locality, they would find their way to the Turkish lines and report our movements.

Enemy aeroplanes visited us occasionally. One afternoon a taube hovered for a few seconds over the lines of a Camel company, then dropped three bombs which crashed down on the bivvies erected at the foot of a sandy ridge. Not one man was injured, although several had narrow escapes from death. Natives attached to the company to attend to sick camels, spent days erecting a bomb-proof shelter. It was a sturdy structure with sandbag walls and roof. Yet, when the taube hovered overhead these same natives, terrified at the noise of the descending bombs, fled toward the open desert, while several Cameliers dashed inside the sandbag shelter.

One afternoon a stifling khamsin swept down upon El Arish,

almost suffocating us as we crouched down in our dugouts. The swirling and gritty sand struck the exposed parts of our bodies like the lash of a whip; soon little streams of blood were trickling down our faces and arms. When the khamsin reached its full force the shifting sand almost buried our dugouts, so we stood out in the open and endeavoured to protect our faces with our arms. The camels also had a bad time. On such occasions they turn their backs to the khamsin and close their nostrils, thus preventing themselves from breathing properly. When the storm had passed two of the camels in my company were dead.

On 8 January the Cameliers had a successful sports meeting at El Arish—successful while it lasted. When a German pilot in a taube passing overhead noticed the gathering he took a keen interest in us. No doubt he wondered why we had gathered there, and why we were so excited. Just as "Stinker" and "Eau-de-Cologne" were running a dead-heat in the Camel Handicap the airman swooped lower. Thinking he was going to drop a bomb we scattered in all directions. That was the end of our sports meeting.

When we returned to our lines, ammunition was being hand-ed out; that meant there was a stunt ahead of us. Soon afterwards we were ordered to have a hurried a meal and then to load the camels with full equipment. Just before dusk we mounted and rode northward from El Arish. It was a general move. Away to-ward the coast we could see long lines of light horsemen and yeomanry moving forward, and behind them came the guns.

"Looks as if it will not be long before we see the Promised Land we used to hear about when we went to Sunday-school," said a long, lean Camelier as he rode up beside me.

"Yes," replied the man behind him. And I suppose that's why they let us hold a sports meeting this afternoon. Wanted us to be in a good humour for a long night ride, and a decent scrap at the end of it."

We did not know our destination: if the officers knew they kept it to themselves.

A light horseman galloped past.

"Hey, where are we going?" yelled Snowy Allen.

"Constantinople," cried the light horseman, without looking back.

The sun disappeared behind the horizon, spreading a vivid rose colour over the western sky—a striking contrast to the dull grey sand over which our camels slowly padded their way. As the twilight deepened, the pulsating heat of the day gave way to a refreshing coolness brought by a fanning breeze which swept toward us from the coast. The stillness of the night grew even more intense. Denied the luxury of a cigarette the hours seemed to drag.

At intervals we halted while more horsemen galloped past us. It was eerie sitting on our camels watching the shadowy forms of man and beast as they moved ahead. If they had stopped a few seconds and told us what was going to happen, and where, we would have felt more satisfied. It did not dawn upon us that the horsemen were probably as ignorant as ourselves concerning our destination.

Just before nine o'clock a rising moon flooded the desert with its pale, searching light. Soon afterwards we received the order to halt and dismount. Ahead of us stood a mud hut.

"The half-way pub, boys," called out Snowy Allen. "What are you drinking?"

"Shut your mouth," came a stern order from Lieutenant Linford, as he walked across to where we were now squatted on the sand.

We had halted at Sheikh Zowaiid, a delightful spot of greenness that showed up in the moonlight. Sinai, with its long days and nights of riding over barren desert sand now lay behind us.

Ahead was the Holy Land.

"Sleep if you want to; we will be here for some time," said an officer.

We barraked our camels and stretched ourselves out on the sand. Few of us closed our eyes. Without waiting for the order we puffed at cigarettes and pipes, and no one stopped us. It was Snowy Allen who gave us the information we desired so much. He had overheard several officers talking, and caught a word uttered here and there.

"Seems the Turks are strongly entrenched somewhere ahead," he said, "and we are to attack them at dawn."

"How many are there?" asked someone.

"Oh, about a million," drawled Snowy, as he removed a blanket from his saddle, and covering himself with it turned over on the sand to get a few hours' sleep before we moved again.

Darkie Fox looked at him. "I bet you'd sleep in the middle of an earthquake."

"Iron nerves, my boy. All my ancestors had them; they were the backbone of the Empire in many a by-gone war."

" Oh yes, I 've read about them on the labels of bully-beef tins."

Allen did not reply. From beneath the blanket came the sound of heavy breathing. The night ride, and what lay ahead, was not troubling him.

Shortly after one o'clock we mounted and followed each other in long straggling lines. The horsemen had disappeared; but to the left of us the Bing Boys were jogging along without uttering a word.

Already we had covered some fifteen miles since we rode out from El Arish; and we rode another ten miles before we came to Magruntein just as dawn was breaking. Here the landscape was covered with stunted bushes; ahead were grassy flats good to look upon after gazing for months at sandy plains and shifting sand-dunes. The camels sniffed the grass and craned their necks forward. It was with difficulty that we held them.

Here we again linked up with several horsemen, some of whom were guarding Bedouin prisoners. Then we knew why these men had raced ahead of us during the night. Bedouins had their encampments scattered about the country between Sheikh Zowaiid and Rafa, so they had to be rounded up and caught before they could warn the Turks that we were approaching. Several of these Bedouins carried rifles and ammunition, no doubt supplied to them by the Turks. As usual they were clad in filthy garments; and it is doubtful if water had touched their bodies for months. As we rode past, hatred of our men showed on their dust-grimed features.

Riding slowly over a grassy plain, we soon came to a cultivated stretch of land where three small Bedouin children stood and watched us with wide-open eyes. We waved to them, and laughingly asked them why they were up so early. We had spoken only a few words when a shell crashed overhead, and shrapnel pellets rained down upon us. Other shells followed in rapid succession. Most of us jumped down from our camels, and, tugging at their reins, persuaded the beasts to follow us out of the danger zone.

Several shells went beyond their objective and burst over the spot where the Bedouin children were standing. Regardless of the danger, a woman rushed out from a mud hut standing in the centre of the farm, and soundly spanking the eldest child she abused him, probably, for not remaining indoors. With shrapnel tearing up the ground around her she picked up the two youngest children and carried them to the hut. At any other time we would have laughed and probably cheered the woman, but now there were more serious things to think about. The enemy gunners had the range; it is surprising that none of our men were killed.

A few minutes later we reached a grassy rise, out of range of shell-fire, and halted. We now had our first opportunity of looking towards the enemy redoubts and noticed several lines of trenches. In the central position there appeared to be half a dozen carefully constructed redoubts arranged in such a way that the enemy could deal with an attack from any quarter. Apparently we had come upon them unawares. Even now many Turks were rushing into the trenches, having been disturbed just as they were about to have breakfast.

What we noticed more than anything else was the open ground over which we would have to advance before we could reach the enemy position. The odds were overwhelmingly against us; everything pointed to the fact that the machine-gunners would mow us down in hundreds. No doubt the same thing was in the minds of the enemy when they prepared this stronghold. Later on, when we advanced, we were to learn that out in front of their trenches were many concealed rifle-pits crowded with picked sharp-shooters. We didn't like our chance of success and told each other so.

Snowy Allen had plucked a blood-red poppy from the grass at his feet—the first flower he had seen for many months. Sticking it in his hat-band, he listened to us for a few minutes, then lit a cigarette, puffed slowly at it, and drawled:

"Did it ever strike you fellows that our 'heads' know what they are doing? I'll wager a month's pay to a tin of *Fray Bentos* that General Chauvel has worked all this out in his head days ago; and he ain't going to order us to advance where the Turks will make a slaughter-yard of us."

"But I thought Sir Archibald Murray was running this little show," countered another Camelier.

"He might be., But take it from me Chauvel has a say in things when it comes to pushing the Cameliers into action. You see, this is how they do it. Murray, Chetwode, Chaytor, Chauvel, and a few other 'heads' get together, with a map in front of them. Then they work it all out. Murray will say: 'I think I'll order the yeomanry to advance at this point,' and Chaytor will chip in with: 'Yes. And my men will attack to the right of them.' Chauvel will look at the map for a couple of minutes, then he will say: 'Oh, yes. And I suppose the light horse can hop into the Turks over there toward the left.' Then he will think some more, and say: 'By Jove, I nearly forgot about those Cameliers. They're as rough as bags, so I suggest they attack in the centre.' That's how it's done, me boys. It's as simple as playing dominoes."

"Spare me days, you're a wonderful bloke to find out things," chipped in Darkie Fox. "It beats me why they didn't keep you at headquarters."

"Good fighting men are always put in the firing-line." Then Snowy picked the now drooping poppy from his hat-band and held it out to Darkie. "Here, press this in your pay-book, then send it to your wife and sixteen kids in Australia."

To our right another company of the Camel Corps were also surveying the landscape in front of them, and commenting on the open ground that lay in front of the enemy redoubts. Then came the order to prepare to advance. Gripping their rifles, and with set faces, the Cameliers moved out in single file. Mick Burke turned to his camel and patted the animal on the neck.

"Farewell, me noble steed. Don't be a damn fool and bolt away before I come back."

Giving the animal another pat with his hand, he moved away with the other men. Down the side of the rise they walked, a silent procession. Reaching the flat ground below, they formed into long lines and began to advance. Beside Mick Burke walked another Camelier, a mere boy, a recent reinforcement from Australia, Fear was in his eyes, and the hand shook that held his rifle. It was his first encounter with the enemy.

"Come on, sonny; this is going to be a walkover for us " said Burke, noticing the lagging footsteps of the lad.

"I'm scared.

"By cripes, and so am I. But on occasions like this it doesn't pay to show it. Hop along, and you'll be harpooning Turks in no time."

Chapter 8

We had only moved forward a few yards when the first Camelier fell. He just lurched forward and crumbled in a heap on the ground. Soon others fell. The enemy machine-gunners were sweeping the ground in front of us, and already it looked as if our casualties were going to be heavy.

It cheered us when we noticed that shells from the Royal Horse Artillery, and the Bing Boys' guns appeared to be doing considerable damage to the enemy trenches. The English and Scottish yeomanry had dismounted, and linking up with us on the left, were advancing as confidently as if they were walking down a city street. A shell burst in the centre of their lines; they halted for a few seconds; then went on again.

When we were half a mile from their trenches the Turks and Germans greeted us with a deadly shell and machine-gun fire. Many more men fell. Seeing it was madness to continue the advance just then, our officers ordered us to lie prone on the ground and take advantage of what cover we could find. With our hands we scraped heaps of sand in front of us and lay behind them. In front, and somewhat to the right of us, stood a solitary tree with dense foliage. That tree was responsible for many of our casualties. A man fourth to the right of me fell forward on his face. Soon afterwards the third man from me tried to raise himself from the ground, then toppled sideways; a moment later the Camelier lying next to me rolled on his back, and a red smudge showed on the front of his tunic.

"There's a sniper at work," said Lieutenant Moylan, who was lying on the ground to the left of me.

"Yes," I answered, "and I'll be the next to go."

I lay there, expecting any moment to fall a victim to the concealed sniper's skilful marksmanship, but nothing happened to me. Later we were told that the sniper had been shot by a light horseman.

I carried a tin of cigarettes into action with me, and had carefully treasured them for such an occasion as this. Lieutenants Moylan and Linford soon began to borrow them; when one was finished we lit another. We had not tasted food since the previous afternoon. Still, hunger did not trouble us; there were other and more serious things to think about.

The three men to my right were still alive, but two were badly wounded. One of them was babbling deliriously; the other motioned to me to give him a cigarette. I held one out to him, but he hadn't the strength to take it out of my hand. I lit it and placed it in his mouth. He puffed at it for a few seconds, then it fell to the ground.

Two of our men, Privates Vanston and Galloway, had secured a stretcher from somewhere, and calmly proceeded to carry our wounded to the rear. This action on their part probably saved the lives of many of these men. Paddy Vanston certainly earned the Military Medal awarded to him many months afterwards for his conduct in this engagement.

Hours passed and still we lay out in the open, wondering when the order would come to rush the trenches. A long narrow rifle-pit in front of the enemy's centre trenches especially interested us. The Bing Boys had fired shell after shell at this particular pit, and the little puffs of smoke bursting over it showed they had the range.

"The poor devils in that trench will be mincemeat when this stunt is finished," said Lieutenant Moylan, as he held out his hand for another cigarette.

I agreed with him. When the enemy surrendered there was not a man alive in this particular pit. At the bottom lay mangled corpses, one on top of the other.

Lying next on the left of Lieutenant Linford was a Lewis machine-gunner named Paul. He and Linford had been pals ever since they first met in No. 4 Company. As we lay there Linford would turn to the machine-gunner every few minutes, and advise him in which direction to use his gun. About three o'clock, after speaking to Moylan, he again turned to say something to Paul. The machine-gunner was lying face down on the sand, and one arm was thrown across the gun.

Linford laughed. "Well, I'm damned if he hasn't gone to sleep. Just imagine a man sleeping in a place like this!"

He leaned across and shook the gunner. Paul did not move. Then the officer rolled him on his side, and a thin stream of blood trickled from the hair covering his forehead. While bending over his gun a bullet had gone through the top of Paul's head and come out on the right side of his neck. Death had been instantaneous; he had not uttered a sound.

The death of the machine-gunner had a strange effect upon Linford. For a few moments he seemed dumbfounded. Then, rising to his knees, he shook his fist in the direction of the enemy trenches.

"You murdering swine!" he yelled.

Several of his men tried to persuade him to lie down again, but he refused to listen to them. Suddenly he jumped to his feet and rushed towards the enemy. He had only gone a few steps when he fell with a bullet through his chest.

We were astonished at the way this officer—so popular with the men in his company—had thrown his life away. An Englishman by birth, he had been in some tight corners before he arrived in Australia and became a police constable. At El Arish at night, while we sat in a group, he had related incidents concerning the days when he was a constable in South Africa, and had helped to capture the notorious Jackson gang of motor bandits. It was a coincidence that Lieutenant Moylan, the officer lying near him, had also been a police constable in Australia before he enlisted. He was soon to follow Linford: he died of fever at Cairo some months later.

Gradually the cordon around the enemy redoubts drew closer. Although we could not see them from where we lay, the New Zealand mounted regiments rode round in a semicircle and, dismounting, attacked the enemy from the north-east. To our right we watched the light horsemen dismount and dash towards the Turkish positions, near where the solitary tree stood, but a vigorous machine-gun fire compelled them to retire. At the same time a German taube bombed the horses they had left some distance behind.

We passed questions along the line to find out how other companies were faring. We were told that Captain McCallum, of No. 15 (New Zealand) Company had been wounded some hours earlier while leading his men forward. There were many willing hands prepared to risk the whining bullets to get him back to the rear where the Red Cross men could attend to him. Tenderly he was placed on a stretcher; but the Angel of Death hovered over it. He lingered for two days. There were tear-dimmed eyes in No. 15 Company when the New Zealanders heard he was dead.

I had "hopped over the top" on the shrub-covered hills of Anzac, and on more than one occasion been one of a wild-eyed yelling mob who had charged across the open at Suvla Bay to take a hastily-burrowed trench, already half full of dead and wounded men. But I would have preferred those thrilling moments to this lying for hours out in the open with only a useless barricade of sand to conceal my face and portion of my body. Ahead were those sandbag covered trenches behind which grim-faced German machine-gunners and experienced Turkish regulars were waiting, finger on trigger, for us to rush forward. The more we stared at those trenches and the open ground that lay between, the more impregnable they seemed to be.

"We've got Buckley's chance of getting within a hundred yards of their first trench," said a man near me.

"Yes," replied another, "the blasted machine-guns would cut us to pieces. It reminds me of the time I was at------"

Here he ducked his head and buried his face in the sand as a bullet chopped up the ground in front of him.

"They won't even let a damned man talk," he muttered as he wiped sand from his eyes and mouth.

I was wondering how Mick Burke was doing. I asked Lieutenant Moylan if he had seen him.

"Yes He's lying a few yards along the line, and be hasn't spoken a word for hours. I think he's got wind up."

"Wind up be damned," snapped Burke, who had overheard the officer's remarks. "Me throat's sore with swallowing acres of sand. It's a great game, this. As soon as I push me head up to see what's doing a swivel-eyed Turk takes a pot-shot at me."

"Serves you right; you were old enough to know what you were doing when you enlisted," said a Camelier behind him.

Burke was about to reply when something else attracted his attention. Towards our left many of the Cameliers were moving. Under Major Bassett, two companies of the 2nd Camel Battalion had left the position they had occupied since they advanced across the open earlier in the day.

"Hullo, our Tommy cobbers are going to hop into the Turks," said a Camelier lying behind me.

"Yes, and I'll wager they'll give Jacko a hell of a time when they get at him with the bayonet," said the man lying next to him.

We had great faith in the fighting abilities of these Tommy comrades of ours in the Camel Corps. Most of them had been transferred from yeomanry units, and they were big sturdy men who could not fail to give a good account of themselves in a hand-to-hand encounter with the enemy.

Lieutenant-Colonel C. L. Smith had just finished instructing Major Bassett what to do with his men when Major Langley, of the 1st Battalion, suggested he order Major H. J. Huddleston to take two companies of the 3rd Battalion, and one company of the 2nd Battalion, and move westward between Bassett's force and the yeomanry, then charge with the bayonet one of the main redoubts in front of them.

Major Huddleston, who was soon to become one of the most popular officers in the Camel Corps, was at this time a stranger to most of us. An Imperial Army officer, he had held the rank of major in the Sudanese Camel Corps before Lieutenant-Colonel Smith selected him to take command of our 3rd Battalion. Before coming to us he had spent many years fighting and patrolling in the Sudan, and was used to every phase of desert warfare. Furthermore, he had a thorough knowledge of the ways of camels, and was a splendid Arabic linguist. To sum him up in a few brief words: he was a born soldier, a leader of men, and the possessor of a charming personality. The men in his battalion soon became greatly attached to him, and would have followed him against overwhelming odds had he desired them to do so. After his shrewd leadership and reckless bravery at Rafa the Cameliers unanimously considered he was a "decent sorter bloke."

The Bing Boys now directed their guns on the redoubt that was the Cameliers' objective, and soon afterwards Major Huddleston ordered his men to charge. With fixed bayonets, and supported by New Zealanders, the Cameliers dashed forward across the open ground determined to reach their objective at any cost. At the same time the remainder of us, now spectators as it were, concentrated our rifle and machine-gun fire on the Turkish redoubts. Soon the New Zealanders with a sweeping rush reached the trenches, and many of the now terrified Turks threw up their arms and surrendered.

Almost at the same moment Huddleston s men dashed toward the southern part of the position, yelling as they ran. Ahead of his men, Captain G. A. Smith, of No. 12 Company, fell mortally wounded. The yelling line charged the redoubt only to be met by exhausted Turks who threw up their arms or raised white flags.

The sight of the flags was the signal for the remainder of us to dash forward. Turks and Germans were now coming out of the trenches like ants. I was half-way across the slope when a light horse officer ordered me to take charge of several prisoners who were following him.

"Get them away as quickly as you can," he said. "Turkish reinforcements are coming."

These prisoners numbered about a hundred men and officers. I ordered them to move quickly, but walking past the spot where they had been about to have their breakfast that morning several of them stopped to pick up food. I yelled to them in Arabic to hurry along but they took no notice of me. Just then an officer stepped from amongst the prisoners and asked me if I could give him a match. With one eye on the lagging men at the rear of the procession I handed him a box of matches, and he held out his cigarette-case. Taking a Turkish cigarette from it I noticed that two of the prisoners were now sitting down eating food.

I'll give you a minute to move, and if you don't do it I am going to shoot to kill," I yelled, forgetting for the moment that these men would not understand the English language. I raised my rifle and covered the two Turks. Noticing my action they rose to their feet, and at the same moment another dapper young officer stepped from amongst the prisoners and walked across to me.

"Don't shoot them," he said in perfect English.

"What the hell are you talking about?" I cried.

The young officer, with a smile on his good-looking face, placed one hand on my shoulder: "My friend, don't you think there has been enough murder here to-day without you killing one of those men? I will speak to them."

He turned and spoke sharply in his own language to the lagging men, and they promptly followed the procession. While he was doing so I noticed the officer to whom I had given the matches had walked back amongst the prisoners. The young officer gazed at his retreating figure, then spat on the ground.

"Damned German!"

"You don't like them?"

"No. I am a Turk, and we do not like them. They are too domineering."

We walked along in silence for a few minutes. Somehow I could not help liking this smiling-faced youth.

"Tell me, friend," he said, stopping for a moment, "where will we be taken from here?"

"Cairo."

"Will the German and Turkish officers have to live in the same prison compound?"

"No."

"Ah, that is good."

By this time long lines of prisoners were streaming from the captured redoubts. The rumour that Turkish reinforcements were coming toward Rafa was the signal for us to get our prisoners away as quickly as possible. As it happened, the reinforcements did not arrive. Not knowing this the Cameliers mounted, and with their prisoners again turned their faces toward El Arish. Darkness was now closing over the battlefield, where some of our men were burying our dead.

Slowly we rode back, and on foot plodded the prisoners. With us were sand carts carrying the wounded. Arriving at Sheikh Zowaiid shortly after midnight we halted and were told we could have something to eat, and also rest for a few hours.

A rum issue was handed round. Snowy Allen missed it; he was away somewhere. When he came back and found there was none left, he expressed himself rather forcibly:

"Well, I'm the stiffest poor cow in this part of the world. If I was in a crowd being issued with wings in heaven, I'd get the last pair that was left, and they would be so mildewed that I couldn't fly with them."

Later in the day we rode into El Arish. Moving to No. 4 Company lines, a Camelier who had been left behind, met the first of his comrades:

"So Linford is dead?"

"Yes. How did you know?"

"Oh, the Gyppos who attend to the sick camels told me. They're funny beggars. Yesterday afternoon they were all seated in a circle along the line there, when suddenly one of them jumped up and began to wail that Linford had just been killed. That started them all wailing, and they've been doing it ever since. Clairvoyance or telepathy, I suppose."

Several days passed before the natives ceased to mourn the loss of lieutenant Linford. They had taught him Arabic, and were greatly attached to the smiling faced young ex-constable.

Chapter 9

Owing to the lengthy period the animals they rode could go without water, the Cameliers, on the fringe of the Holy Land, often found themselves detailed for lengthy patrols that could not have been undertaken by mounted horsemen. They attacked several isolated Turkish garrisons, and at the end of these long and lonely rides, far from the actual scene of hostilities, returned with many prisoners. At other times they had occasional skirmishes with prowling bands of Bedouins, armed with Turkish rifles. Although these were minor affairs, they assisted to keep our flanks clear of spies who otherwise would have kept the enemy well informed concerning the movements of the main bodies of troops.

The Flying Corps reported that there was a small Turkish garrison at Bir el Hassana, thirty odd miles south-west of Magdhaba, and Sir Archibald Murray, Commander of the Expeditionary Force on this front, felt sure it was a little job that could safely be left to the Cameliers. The 2nd Battalion, consisting of Tommies, and in charge of Major Bassett, moved out from Magdhaba on the evening of 17 February, and rode all night. It was another of those dreary night rides when men spoke in whispers, and no smoking was allowed. Still, the men of the 2nd Battalion did not mind; they were rather pleased at having this little job all to themselves.

"By goom," whispered a sturdy Tommy, mounted on a big, shaggy-looking camel, "we'll show those Anzacs in the other companies how we can put the fear of the Lord into a crowd of Turks when we attack them."

"Haven't we been doing that ever since we left the blinking Canal?" muttered the man riding beside him.

"Yes, and we're not getting six bob a day for it either," growled another Tommy.

The night passed slowly with weary khaki-clad men whispering and mumbling about anything that came into their minds. It helped to keep them awake. Occasionally a halt was ordered, and those in the rear wondered what was happening ahead. Then on again, to halt for another interval after travelling a few miles. Once a cacolet became unfastened on the back of a camel. Then the animal, probably half asleep, snorted and tore wildly down a narrow wady, with the ambulance stretcher dangling behind his hind-legs.

After much wasted time, and many oaths that stabbed the stillness of night, the alarmed camel was pacified and the cacolet again fixed to its proper place on his back. Then the procession again moved forward.

These cacolet-laden animals always accompanied the Camel Corps into action, and carried the wounded to the nearest hospital or dressing-station. A ride in a cacolet was an experience that was not soon forgotten by the wounded men who were carried in it. Each camel carried two cacolets, one fastened to each side of a saddle made specially for the purpose. They resembled a stretcher-bed with a low rail surrounding it, and were covered with a calico hood to keep the sun off from the wounded occupant. If a heavier man happened to be in the opposite cacolet the stretchers would each sway up and down see-saw fashion, with the result that the men lying in them would be tossed violently against the railing or almost thrown to the ground. To a badly wounded man the motion over a long distance was the very refinement of torture. Still it had to be endured as there was no other way of getting him to hospital.

Dawn was breaking when the Cameliers came in sight of Bir el Hassana. A sleepy-eyed Turkish sentry was the first to notice the long straggling lines of camel-men who came from nowhere as it were, their legs crossed over the necks of the animals they rode, while they held their rifles in a lazy sort of way, but ready if the necessity arose.

The sentry rubbed his eyes to make sure he was not the victim of an early-morning mirage, then he alarmed the little garrison, and soon half-clad Turks were hurrying in all directions. The Cameliers gripped their rifles more firmly, but seeing they were outnumbered the Turks threw up their hands and surrendered. A Tommy sergeant strolled across to where a small Turkish flag was fluttering from a stick stuck in the sand, tore it down, and ground it under his heel. A surly-faced Turk endeavoured to pick it up, and rolled his eyes protestingly at the other's impetuosity. He raised his rifle as if to shoot.

"You son of a thousand pigs," snarled the sergeant, as his arm shot out; the Turk's legs sagged at the knees, then he fell in a heap on the sand. That sergeant had lost his only brother at Rafa, and he was disappointed that the men in the garrison were not going to make a fight of it.

If the Turks had not the heart to fight it was different with a small band of armed Bedouins camped in their camel-hair tents on the outskirts of the garrison. They fired from a distance at the Cameliers; but their marksmanship was erratic, and none of our men were injured.

A patrol was sent out to round up these desert nomads, but when they approached close to them a Bedouin fired at close range, and Lance-corporal MacGregor fell badly wounded. He was carried back to the garrison, but owing to the nature of his wound it was found impossible to convey him to hospital in a cacolet, so one of our planes flying overhead was signalled to and descended. MacGregor had his wound roughly dressed, then he was placed in the observer's seat and the plane flew direct to El Arish. It was an incident unique in the history of the mounted units on that front; no other wounded man was conveyed to a field-hospital in quicker time.

Later in the day a party of silent, grim-faced Cameliers captured the Bedouin who had shot the lance-corporal. They didn't waste much time with him. With picks, shovels, and rifles they marched out to a sandy hillock, and the Bedouin was forced to go with them. Half an hour later they returned—without the Bedouin.

The Cameliers were accustomed to the filth of these scattered garrisons, but Bir El Hassana was worse than any they had yet visited. A dead camel lay in the centre of the village, and a dead cow in a building close by. The mud huts were infested with fleas, and clouds of flies hovered around any particle of food lying about the place. And the Turks looked as if water had not touched them or their clothing since the outbreak of hostilities in Sinai.

The next of these minor operations in which the Cameliers took a leading part was the capture of Nekhl, a garrison settlement perched on the heights of a desert range to the south of Sinai. This garrison interfered little with the progress of our troops toward the Holy Land, but the Bedouins, who were still troublesome in these parts, had to be impressed with the strength and fighting abilities of the invading army that had fought its way from the Canal and were now moving towards Gaza.

To capture Nekhl, a yeomanry regiment moved out from Suez. At the same time the 11th Light Horse Regiment, and one company of the Imperial Camel Corps rode from Serapeum. Towards the east Major Bassett's Cameliers waited to stop the retreat from Nekhl, should the inhabitants of that lofty settlement attempt to flee at the approach of the British troops.

Prowling Bedouins watched the armed horse and camel men riding through the wadies and over the rugged hills. They lost no time in finding their way back to Nekhl and warning those within the garrison that enemy troops were approaching. The Turks prepared to evacuate the settlement, but while they were doing so a keen-eyed airman hovering overhead in one of our planes noticed their movements, and flying back informed the leader of the light horse regiment that if he did not hurry forward he would find only a deserted garrison.

The camels, urged on by the heels of their riders, moved faster over the uneven sand. While still a great distance away the Australians saw Nekhl, then soon discerned a mosque surrounded by several stone huts. The light horsemen, followed by the Cameliers, spread out in a half-circle, fully expecting those within this lofty garrison to put up some sort of resistance. Once again they were disappointed. A few surly-faced Turks and crafty-looking Bedouins came forward to surrender. The Australians searched the huts, but wasted no time in getting away from them. Heat, flies, sights, and smells, were much the same as at Bir el Hassana.

After these minor operations the different Camel companies spent monotonous weeks between Rafa and Sheikh Nuran, and they were mostly responsible for outpost duty in the vicinity of their camping-grounds. There were some thrilling and humorous incidents conected with these outposts. Just before we moved toward Sheikh Nuran, the company to which I had now transferred, almost daily, after dusk, sent four men in charge of an N.C.O. out to certain posts. Taking blankets with us re would walk, perhaps three or four miles, until just ahead of us were the enemy positions. Here we would stay till day was about to break, each man doing a two-hour watch; then we would return to our lines.

One morning, after a dreary night, we were preparing to return to our lines when we noticed several horsemen galloping from a ehain of sandhills about three miles away, where the enemy were strongly entrenched. We knew the Turks had two brigades of cavalry behind their lines, so we concluded that these were some of them about to raid our outposts. We had no chance against such a force, but in a few seconds discussed if we would make a fight of it or surrender.

"Prisoners break stones in the streets of Aleppo," said a tall, wrinkled Camelier.

"Yes," said another "and they knock the stuffing out of them if they don't do it."

We decided to fight. When the horsemen approached closer, still coming at full gallop, we piled sand upon us and lay behind it: we could drop a few of them out of their saddles before they got us. The N.C.O. was about to order us to fire when he got up and stared hard at the approaching horsemen. There was a look of amazement on his face; then it gave way to a wide grin.

"Well, I'm jiggered. They're New Zealanders!"

We all laughed, greatly relieved. A few seconds before we had expected to be shot down after a brief exchange of rifle-fire.

Our N.C.O. went forward to speak to the good-looking young lieutenant who was leading the New Zealanders.

"We were about to open fire on you, sir. We would have done it had I not noticed the hats you were wearing as you approached closer."

"But why should you fire on us?"

"We thought you were Turks out to raid our outposts."

The lieutenant threw one leg over the front of his saddle, and there was the shadow of a smile on his face.

"Were you not informed before you left your lines yesterday that we were sending out a mounted patrol early this morning?"

"Never heard a word about it."

"I'll have to inquire into this. Every unit about here should have been notified. As a matter of fact we went out hoping to coax some of these mounted Turks into the open, but they were not having it on. Are you fellows good shots?"

"Yes, we're pretty good."

"Well then, it was just as well you didn't fire at us," laughed the lieutenant as he led his men back to their lines.

On another occasion I was detailed for a rather risky job. Anzacs were usually selected for tasks with an element of danger attached to them. The first day I joined up with No. 3 Company at Mersa Matruh, Captain Naylor happened to glance at my pay-book.

"So you were at Gallipoli. You are the sort of fellow I want."

At times I regretted ever going to Gallipoli.

This particular duty for which I was detailed meant locating the exact whereabouts of a sniper who was supposed to be concealed in a vast clump of shrubbery, a mile in front of where we were bivouacked and extending back to the enemy's position.

"We've got an idea a sniper is concealed there," said the officer, giving me final instructions, "and we believe he is watching our movements. I want you to creep around the front of that shrubbery. If you see him you are to return here and report; we will then send a larger force out to get him. You can take Ryan with you."

I looked at Ryan. He was a recent reinforcement from Australia, and I would have preferred someone with more experience in desert warfare. As we moved away from the lines the officer who had given me my instructions called out:

"I'll have my glasses on both of you, and if you get into trouble I'll send some of the men to your assistance.''

"Yes," muttered Ryan, "and by that time the flamin' sniper will have filled us with lead."

We walked slowly toward a tree about three hundred yards from the front of the shrubbery. Here we stopped for several minutes and discussed the best way to approach our destination. Then, on hands and knees, and dragging our rifles behind us we crawled towards the bushes.

We reached them and again rested. Peering between them we could see no sign of a sniper. Behind those bushes were other bushes, and yet others, completely concealing what was behind them. We crawled along, peering into the bushes every few yards. I was in front, with Ryan close behind me. Suddenly an icy dullness ran down my spine: I was looking down the barrel of a rifle. Behind it was the unshaven face of a Turk.

Many thoughts flashed through my brain at that moment. I was about to raise the rifle beside me, but quickly abandoned the idea. I thought of jumping to my feet and running, but knew I would not go far before the Turk would drop me.

'' Get a move on," said Ryan.

I wanted to tell him that a Turk had me covered, but although I opened my mouth no words came. I kicked backwards and my boot struck Ryan in the face.

"What the hell do you think you are doing?"

I kicked out the other leg, and his head went back with a jerk.

''Wow! You fat-headed fool, you nearly brained me."

Taking no notice of him I began to creep backwards, inch by inch, and ever so slowly until my face was close to that of the man who had been behind me.

"Go for your life," I whispered. "There's a Jacko covering us with his rifle."

"Where?" asked Ryan.

"You'll damned soon know where if you don't get a move on," I whispered, my mouth almost touching his ear. "He's behind that bush in front of us."

Just then Ryan caught sight of the end of the rifle-barrel, and bounding to his feet, raced away in the direction of the tree where we had rested. I followed, and we both reached the tree together.

Seeing that something unusual had happened, the officer who had been watching us from our lines, sent several men at the double to our assistance. We pointed to where the sniper was concealed, then in a body we advanced toward the bushes.

The sniper had disappeared.

There was the spot where he, and probably others, had watched our movements for days. Judging by the number of empty rifle-shells lying around, no doubt they had done much of the sniping that had worried our patrols since we arrived in the locality. It was an admirable place for a sniper, and under cover of the dense shrubbery at the rear he had no difficulty in returning unseen to his lines. Probably, the reason he did not fire at Ryan and me was because he knew if he did so it would have resulted in our guns shelling his sniping-possie before he had a chance to escape.

Chapter 10

The first faint flush of dawn was showing in the east as we rode from Sheikh Zowaiid, and it was pleasant travelling. The wide desert sand was behind us, and it was good to gaze once more upon rolling plains of green vegetation. Our joy at sight of barley-fields and flowering plants was similar, no doubt, to that of the Israelites who, after forty years' wandering in the wilderness reached the Promised Land.

When we turned our backs on Sheikh Zowaiid, where we had rested during the past few weeks, we knew that there was a big "stunt" ahead of us. Night after night there was a moving of troops; as fast as one brigade left another marched in and took its place. Turkish scouting-planes visited us daily, hovered over our lines for a few minutes, until they found out what they wanted to know, then flew back to their aerodromes without dropping anything to remind us there was a war on. Still, the sight of a black-tailed taube above sent us scurrying in all directions like frightened rabbits. As one Camelier—a 1914 man—said:

"A fellow has a chance when he is fighting on the ground, but when a bomb drops from above, and we happen to be anywhere near where it lands, the odds are dead against us."

Approaching Rafa we came on long straggling lines of Tommies, dusty and leg weary. These men of the 2nd Lowland Infantry Division, after fighting at Gallipoli had marched and fought right across Sinai. We liked these Scotties, and were glad they were going to be with us when we attacked Gaza.

We rode up alongside them, and they grinned at us, although it was a weary sort of smile.

"Where are you going, Jock?" asked a Camelier, as he

stopped his camel beside a sturdy Scotsman, bent under the weight of a full haversack.

"Oh, we've got an appointment with Abdul in Gaza, and it's going to be a swell affair. You had better come along."

"You bet your sweet life we'll be there."

We chatted with these fighting-men for several minutes, then rode on. It was after dark when we came to Hassan-el-Kebir. Here we had a hurried meal, then stretched ourselves on the ground to rest, still fully equipped and with our rifles beside us. It would not be long before we moved. Away toward Gaza the big guns were already disturbing the stillness of night; the air was full of swift shells that whined and hissed before they landed with a deafening crash inside the town.

We were aroused at 1 a.m., and after stern orders from our officers not to strike matches, again mounted our camels and rode through thick fog. It was so dense that we could hardly see the men riding in front of us. Soon afterwards we came to the Wady Ghuzze, which was a narrow, steep-sided river-bed. Here we dismounted, and leading the camels in single file, crossed over to Tel el Jemmi, one of three huge hills, each artificially built in the form of a double cross by the Crusaders in bygone years.

It was eerie waiting there in the darkness, not knowing where we were or what was to happen. Away on our left the big guns were still hurling shells; then came the rat-tat-tat of machine-guns. A chilly breeze came before dawn, and then a sickly sun peered over the eastern horizon. The fog was still heavy, but in the distance we could discern mounted men and infantry moving forward. Behind us an English battery seemed to be waiting, as we were, for orders to move.

A long, lean officer walked amongst us, exchanging a few words with those who cared to speak. At this time a stranger to most of us, only a few weeks were to pass before Lieutenant-Colonel N. B. de Lancey Forth was to prove himself one of the most heroic officers in the Imperial Camel Corps. He had taken charge of the 3rd Battalion back at Rafa, replacing Major Huddleston, who had been transferred to a Tommy brigade of infantry.

We were sorry when Huddleston left the battalion, but a man of such outstanding ability was not allowed to remain with us. He had been decorated for his reckless bravery during the battle of Rafa, and when he rode along our lines to bid farewell to all of us he said in a shaky voice:

"I was awarded the D.S.O. for the Rafa engagement. But I did not win it: you boys won it for me."

When we made a few inquiries about de Lancey Forth we concluded he might be a worthy successor to Huddleston. He was a Victorian native who had served in the Boer War as a trooper with a Queensland Bushmen's Contingent. Later he obtained a commission in the Imperial Army, and for some years was a cavalry officer. Eventually he joined the Sudanese Camel Corps. With this unit he secured a perfect knowledge of camel work. That probably was the reason why Lieutenant-Colonel Smith, V.C., selected him to command our battalion in succession to Huddleston.

At nine o'clock the fog suddenly lifted, and we could plainly see the 53rd Division moving toward Ali Muntar Ridge. Behind them came ambulance-carts drawn by mules, and camels with white-hooded cacolets swaying unevenly on their backs. Then came armoured-car batteries, and horse artillery. Out on the flanks mounted men were moving. It was a wonderful sight; none of us had seen anything like it before.

"I've wanted to see a decent scrap ever since I left Australia," said Jack Condon, "and this looks like the real thing."

"There's no doubt about it," replied Sergeant Bolton Wood, who was squatted on his heels. "But I wonder when we are going to hop into the business."

"We'll be right in the middle of it before the day is over," drawled Doc Wright.

"Of course we will," said Tommy Byers. "How are they going to win a battle without the Camel Corps?"

So far as we could see from where we were watching the scene of battle there was little doing before noon. Then we were ordered to move to Khurbet el Aseiferiyeh, and watch that Turkish reinforcements did not advance between there and Huj. Stationed on a ridge, we watched the infantry attacking Ali Muntar, where Samson had carried the gates of Gaza close on two thousand years previously. In front of the Tommies were cactus hedges through which they had to hack their way with bayonets while the Turks mowed them down with rifle and machine-gun fire. The infantry fell in hundreds but still they went on. They had already taken Mansura and Sheluf, but ahead of them were many cleverly concealed machine-guns, and heavy guns were hidden in rocky hollows. The Tommies had a frightful time. Their scattered lines were not only swept with rifle and machine-gun fire, but with shrapnel and high-explosive shells. Before the infantry reached the bottom of the hill the ground behind them was black with dead and wounded men. When they reached the summit some battalions had been almost wiped out, and those who still fought were completely exhausted.

At 5 p.m. we received orders to put our camels under cover. Then we went forward on foot to cover the retirement of the yeomanry and light horse. We were beginning to feel the cold. At midnight we received orders to retire to our camels, and when we reached them, to mount without making any noise. Anyone acquainted with the ways of camels will understand how difficult it was to carry out such an order. With gurgling snorts, and bubbling fretfully, the animals took their own time in getting to their feet, then they tossed their shaggy heads and uttered a series of husky croaks. The noise they made could have been heard miles away. Once we got them going they trotted in silence, and we rode until early morning.

At daylight we saw the light horse retiring with shells bursting over them. The attack upon Gaza had been a failure! We couldn't understand it. Throughout the night scraps of information concerning the movements of our troops had reached us. We had been told that the Australian and New Zealand mounted troops had fought their way right through Gaza, and that at all points the enemy were on the run with mounted men and infantry following close behind them.

"Well, if this is a victory, I'll kiss my camel," said a sleepy-eyed Camelier, shading his eyes with one hand as he gazed toward Gaza.

Then came long strings of men too exhausted to care what was happening. Mounted, and on foot, they passed us. A light horse ambulance galloped away to our right. One horse was practically dead in the shafts, and the others were dragging him along. A shell burst close by and the driver toppled from his seat. He rose to his feet and started to run after the ambulance. There was the whine of another shell, then something struck the base of his throat. Wavering on his legs and clawing at his neck, he went down in a heap.

Men who had lost their horses stumbled along wearily, and others slumbered in their saddles. It was an army that slept as it moved. Sometimes a man fell from his horse and lay on the ground until someone picked him up and assisted him to mount again. Ambulance camels with swaying cacolets trotted over the uneven ground led by Egyptian drivers who had their heads shrouded in blankets. No one spoke to us as they passed. They were too exhausted to talk. All they wanted was sleep.

We again mounted and rode to the south of Gaza. Soon afterwards we came upon a large body of Turks concealed in a barley-field. We approached to within tour thousand yards of them, then our company was sent forward to draw their fire so that we could locate their exact whereabouts. At two thousand yards the Turks opened fire on us, but we quickly took shelter in the wadies around us. There we returned the fire with such accuracy that the enemy thought it safer not to show themselves.

Shells now began to burst overhead; our own artillery were

firing at us, thinking we were Turks. We retired to the battalion. Here, under cover of a low hill, we had a hasty meal, then the battalion moved forward to engage the enemy.

The fighting that followed was exciting, and the casualties of the enemy were heavy, stopping their advance. Lieutenant "Jock" Davidson, of No. 12 Company, who was directing the fire of our machine-guns, showed great daring. Just before dusk, the Turkish artillery opened fire on us. Once again we retired, leaving three machine-gunners, Corporal Johns, Doc Wright and Tommy Byers, who were to collect the empty Lewis-gun pans, and then rejoin their company the best way they could. While they were endeavouring to do this, the enemy opened fire on them. Those Turks knew the range and were no novices with a rifle. Cautiously keeping under cover the three men crawled inch by inch towards the rear. Johns was about to order the men to dash for a nearby wady, when a bullet zipped close by his head. His eyes narrowed as he gazed at the furrow of the bullet in the sand:

"We'll have to make a break for it. Those fellows over there will soon wipe us out with a shell if we stay here. Come on! Run like hell!"

The three men jumped into it almost at the same moment. As they did so, a 5.9 shell burst overhead. When the smoke and dust had cleared, Johns was standing upright against the steep bank. He was unconscious, and a thin stream of blood ran from his mouth.

There was the screech of another shell, and Wright and Byers threw themselves face downward on the floor of the wady. The shell burst some distance away. After waiting a while for another, that didn't come, they went across to where Johns was still standing. Seeing he was not dead, they carried him down the wady; then, after a certain amount of rough handling by the two men, he opened his eyes. Concussion plays strange tricks with men in battle, but in this instance Johns soon recovered.

Out of range of the Turkish fire, the two machine-gunners, carrying Johns, found their way back to the company. They were about to mount when the Turks began to shell them. Several men and camels were wounded. Captain Rae was standing on a small rise, reporting the recent movements of his company to Lieutenant-Colonel Smith, who was standing beside him, when a shell burst some distance away. The nose-cap whizzed through the air and struck Rae in the back, killing him instantly.

On the right of No. 12 Company other Camel Corps units were still engaging the enemy, but retiring slowly to join us. Then in a body we rode towards Deir el Belah. After riding for what seemed to be hours, we stopped near a field dressing-station. Wounded men on stretchers and on the ground were sitting or lying everywhere, while doctors worked at high pressure on the broken humanity within the tent.

Here Tommy infantry, with swollen tongues, pleaded for water. There was little of the precious fluid left in our tanks, but we could not refuse these heroes of Ali Muntar. We gave them what we could spare, and they gulped down greedily the first water some of them had tastfed since the morning of the previous day.

One sleepy-eyed Camelier had dismounted from his camel to give a drink of water to a long, lean Tommy. Half-filling his mess-tin, the Tommy sat on the ground and slowly swallowed it. The Camelier also sat on the ground and watched him out of half-shut eyes in a head that nodded lower and lower. Then he fell forward, asleep: soon he was snoring. The Tommy finished his water, then went to sleep beside the Australian.

Another Australian had poured water from his tank into the dented crown of his hat, and with it washed his aching feet. He was about to throw it on the ground when two Tommies rushed up, took the hat from the Camelier, and swallowed the water.

Later in the day we camped on a flat at Deir el Belah, where there was no shortage of drinking-water. We had given much of our food to the Tommies on the way from the field of battle, and now found ourselves with little or nothing to eat. The issue of bully and biscuits we had expected when we reached our destination did not materialize. However, the Cameliers were not the sort of men to go hungry, if it could possibly be avoided. Doc Wright and Tommy Owens, of No. 12 Company, went for a stroll, and eventually came to the beach where ships were discharging cargo. Prowling round, they found many cases of tinned meat and other foodstuffs piled up there. But a Tommy was guarding the stack, and he had a bayoneted rifle to assist him in doing it. Further, he did not look to be the sort of man who would let anyone take anything from the stack unless he had a written permit to do so.

Two hungry Cameliers viewed the stack from all sides, scratched their heads and examined it further. Then Doc went over and started to talk to the guard. He praised the courage of the heroic infantry at Ali Mun-ar. Such compliments coming from an Australian were strange to the Tommy. He became keenly interested, and Doc had more to say about the reckless bravery of the infantry at Gaza.

"Every blanky one of them should get a V.C.," said the Camelier.

The Tommy agreed with him.

Out of the corner of one eye Doc watched Owens remove a case of meat from the rear of the stack and carry it away into the curtain of darkness surrounding the food-dump. When he again returned toward the stack, Doc became more enthusiastic about the khaki-clad lads who had scaled the historic heights of Ali Muntar:

"Do you know what? Give me a brigade of those Tommies of yours and I'll take Gaza in a couple of hours."

"By goom, yes. But the Australians would have to be in it, too. We couldn't do without the light horse, choom, or the New Zealand mounted men."

"Perhaps you are right." Then noticing Owens had removed a few more cases from the stack, Doc waved a friendly hand to the Tommy.

"Well, cheerio, old chap. If we ever meet in Cairo, we'll have a bottle or two of the best."

"You bet we will," replied the Tommy. And sloping his rifle, he renewed his sentry-go.

When Doc and Owens returned to camp with the boxes of meat and biscuits, we welcomed them with open arms, and then enjoyed the first decent meal for forty hours.

Chapter 11

After the first attack on Gaza the Imperial Camel Corps became a fighting force of considerable strength, as there were now four battalions in the field. Furthermore, they had become the most cosmopolitan unit in Sinai and Palestine. Most white nationalities were now represented in it, and the majority of them were "hard cases." We probably received no finer tribute than that which was given us by Colonel P. de Piepape, O.C., of the French-Palestine contingent at Rafa toward the latter end of 1917. Addressing the Cameliers on that occasion he said:

The Imperial Camel Corps companies compare with our own Foreign Legion in regard to the diversity of nationalities amongst its members. Also the similarity is carried further in its wonderful fighting qualities.

In addition to the varied collection of British, Dominion, and Indian members in the Corps there was an Italian—a good soldier—who distinguished himself in several engagements before he was transferred to the Intelligence Bureau, where he was detailed for secret service. There was also an Argentino, of Scottish-Spanish blood, whose ambition was to get close enough to the enemy so that he could "clean some of them up with the bayonet." And we had with us a Syrian who had been brought to Broken Hill as a child. While he was with the Cameliers he made no secret of the fact that he was keen to avenge a long-standing blood feud with the Turks.

In one company there was a Russian who always went to the off-side of a camel to mount, and fell off with great regularity. A reckless fighter, he was wounded on several occasions. In our ranks, too, was a Frenchman—a bloodthirsty individual—who had travelled all over the globe, including Canada, the Yukon diggings, and the South Sea Islands. He had his own reasons for not returning to his native land and fighting there. Jews were well represented in the Corps. There was also a Scottish soldier of fortune who had been gun-running for many revolutions in Central and South America. During such disturbances he always took a hand in the fighting. There was a price on his head in more than one capital of a Latin republic.

Behind the lines, it was quite a common occurrence to see a group of Cameliers discussing some subject in a rest camp. Scottish, Welsh, English, Irish, Australians, New Zealanders, and Indians—all would join in the conversation. One Sunday morning, shortly after the first attack on Gaza, such a group were seated on the beach at Deir el Belah, and the conversation drifted into an argument as to which was the most religious unit in the Camel Corps.

"Well," said a Scottish Camelier, "the good old Covenanter Scotchbyterians observed their religion well."

"Perhaps so," admitted a Camelier from Manchester. "But the Anglicans were well trained in their youth, and went to church regularly."

"Let me tell you that you cannot beat an R.C. Irishman for sticking to his church," said a Tommy, whose address had been Limerick before the outbreak of war.

The Australians and New Zealanders said they did not follow any church, in fact, they doubted if they were even Christians.

"You can all have your say," drawled Snowy Allen. "But we Australians reckon these Indians observe their religion the best. They never neglect to pray, no matter how thick the bullets are flying, or how fast the shells are coming."

Several of the group then turned to two dusky Bing Boys who had listened attentively to the discussion.

"I say, Johnnie," remarked a New Zealander, "what do you Indians think about it?"

"All Indiamen think Australians in the Camel Corps are most religious men," replied one of the Bing Boys.

His opinion was greeted with roars of laughter, and a chorus of: "What, those heathens?"

"Yes," said the Indian, "Australian Camel Corps most religious men. Soon as they finish fight they all go to church. All stand round in big ring. Holy man, he stand in the middle of ring; he talk, and he talk, and he talk. Then another holy man he go into ring; he take two holy coins and he throw them up high. All Australian Camel men look up to heaven and say: ' Good God;' then bow down, look on ground, and say: 'Jesus Christ, he's headed them again.'"

However, resting at Deir el Belah was not all arguing about religion and other things. We washed camels, and attended to any minor injuries they had received during the attack on Gaza. There was one brute in our company that did not take kindly to water; in fact, he did not like anything that was done for his welfare. There was a story attached to this particular animal. Back at Sheikh Zowaiid, before we moved toward Gaza, a grazing picket went out with twenty-five camels and returned later in the day with one animal missing. The three men sent out to keep a watchful eye on the animals had passed away time playing cards, and that was probably when the animal took it into his stupid head to wander away.

To lose a camel was a serious matter, in fact, it was a common saying amongst the Cameliers that greater value was placed upon one of these smellful animals than there was upon a fighting man.

"Lose a camel and they are liable to shoot you," said Mick Burke. "But lose yourself and all you'll get is fourteen days in Abbassia clink."

Lieutenant Davidson made no secret of the fact that he was annoyed at the loss of the camel; he told the three men responsible for its loss that if they did not soon find it there would be a few lines of red ink in their pay-books.

Two of the Cameliers, who should have watched that the animal did not wander away, knew something would have to be done; so that night they visited the lines of the Camel Transport Corps, and when the guard was absent, selected the smallest animal they could see and returned with him to our lines. Here, by means of heated hoop-iron, they marked him with No. 12 Company's brand, and rubbed dirt into it to give it an aged appearance. Then they reported to Lieutenant Davidson that they had found the lost animal in the middle of a luxurious barley-field some miles away.

The following morning an officer from the Camel Transport Corps came to our lines looking for a camel. He inspected the brutes in our camp, but seeing they all carried our company's brand, he went to look elsewhere. Three serious-faced Came-liers, who had not taken their eyes off him while he walked up and down our lines, breathed a sigh of relief.

On 30 March we turned our backs on Deir el Belah and rode towards Khan Yunis. We were not sorry. Many things had annoyed us in that grassy camp by the beach; at night mosquitoes disturbed our slumbers; and so did the croaking of frogs in a nearby lagoon where camels and horses were watered.

So far as the mosquitoes were concerned, we were more fortunate than our Tommy comrades. We lit manure fires to keep them away. Such a thing was unknown to the Tommies until Snowy Allen strolled across to their lines and told them about it:

"Of course, you don't want to let the world know about it," he whispered hoarsely to several Tommies who had closely watched him make a manure fire. "As a matter of fact, my old dad back in Australia was the first man to invent these fires. He'd be greatly annoyed if he knew I was letting out the secret to everyone I meet over here."

That afternoon the Tommies gathered much horse manure, and at night many smoke fires were burning in their lines.

The next day we came to a gently undulating plain, in the centre of which nestled the ancient and historic village of Khan Yunis. It was a glorious sight after gazing for months on the aching barrenness of the desert. The country surrounding the village was a panorama of waving barley-crops, swaying palms and almond-trees.

We were not allowed to remain long in this smiling village, which marked the southern boundary of the Land of Goshen. A few hours later we were slowly riding along the cactus-fringed caravan road winding away to the north, and soon afterwards bivouacked at an abandoned Turkish position, with many miles of carefully prepared trenches and gun-pits. It was another barren spot. The days were almost insufferably hot; the soft alluvial dust churned up by the trotting camels rose in suffocating clouds.

Turkish airmen now began to take a keen interest in our movements. Daily they hovered over our lines, and occasionally dropped bombs which did little damage. One morning I, with another Camelier, was detailed to take several camels back to Khan Yunis for water. We rode on either side of the animals to prevent them breaking away. Approaching Khan Yunis, they were liable to break away when they smelt the young barley.

We had covered half the distance when a taube swooped down over us. Leaving the camels we raced zigzag fashion across the open country. The plane followed us and swooped lower until we could see the heads of the two men seated in it. Every moment we expected to be shot out of our saddles. No doubt the men seated in the machine laughed heartily at the dodging antics of the two scared Cameliers below them. Apparently they were only on an observation jaunt, and carried no bombs or machine-gun. Still, if it was their intention to "put the wind up us," they certainly succeeded in doing it.

While bivouacked on the old Turkish position, we were issued with fresh meat and bread. It was a welcome change from the bully and biscuits we had had at every meal for many months past. The days grew monotonous with the watering of camels and patrolling in the direction of Sheikh

Nuran. We occasionally saw Turkish cavalry patrols in the distance, but they did not allow us to get close enough to fire at them.

One morning gas-helmets were issued to us. They were the P.H. type, used in the early days of the war. A rumour went around the camp that the enemy were going to put gas over us any moment. That made us treat the helmets with great respect. Then we were informed we were to assemble at a certain spot where cylinders of gas were to be released. At a given signal we were to fit on our helmets and dash through the gas cloud.

Lieutenant Lennon, an Imperial Officer, was in charge of the gas experiment, and assisting him were three Australian sergeants, Barton, Wilson, and Rountree. The signal to fix helmets and dash through the gas were the words, "Smoke bomb." As soon as we heard them we wasted no time in racing through it without any of us suffering any ill effects. The Bing Boys, however, bivouacked on the bank of a wady, a quarter of a mile away, had a very different experience. They took a keen interest in all that was taking place, and derived much amusement from it until a gust of wind blew the gas in their direction. Jumping to their feet they raced along the sides of the Nady, at the same time unwinding and throwing away their turbans in their frantic efforts to cover their heads with the helmets. It was our turn to laugh. For days afterwards we unmercifully twitted the Indians about their hasty retreat from the gas.

A sick camel on our line was the next subject for experiment. Discharging a cylinder the animal was soon enveloped. When the gas lifted we expected to find a dying camel, but much to our surprise the animal walked away quite unconcerned. And his ailment, whatever it had been, was completely cured; the following day when a Camelier rode him out on a patrol, he was as lively as any other camel in the Corps.

Our next move was back to the beach at Rafa, where we remained for a few days. Late one afternoon, without the slightest warning, a queer monster of grotesque shape, and emitting strange noises, came rumbling across the sand in our direction. The camels became so alarmed that they broke away from their lines.

"Spare me days if it ain't a blanky big turtle," said a Camelier, after staring for several seconds at the uncouth object.

This was our first sight of a tank. We had heard much about these monstrous engines of war, and were overjoyed at their arrival, believing that as soon as they went into action they would strike terror in the ranks of the enemy.

Turkish airmen now began to drop messages requesting us to remove our hospitals lest they be hit by bombs intended to destroy food or ammunition-dumps. It was regrettable that many of our field-dressing stations and hospitals were near these dumps. We took no notice of the messages, with the result that one night an enemy plane dropped several bombs on an ammunition-dump at Deir el Belah, and a hospital marquee, full of sick and wounded men, was completely destroyed.

The second night we were at Rafa Turkish planes flew over the camp and dropped three bombs. Six men were killed and many others wounded. Hearing the planes approaching, most of the men in camp rushed toward the beach, and this is where the casualties took place. Evidently those in the bombing-machines followed the shoreline, as the edge of the water presented a better target than did the dark clumps of trees surrounding the camp.

After bombing Rafa the planes proceeded toward El Arish. Earlier in the day one of the enemy machines hovered over this now busy military base, and dropping a bomb on a party of Egyptian labourers, killed thirty and wounded many others. When the taubes again came over at night and dropped bombs the only casualty was an Egyptian, who was smothered when his dugout, on the side of a sandhill, caved in. However, the frayed nerves of the dusky labourers could not stand any further aerial raids. When dawn broke the following morning some of them were ten miles away, hurrying back towards the Canal. Indian mounted troops were sent in pursuit. They brought back several of the terrified deserters, but the desert railway now approaching Rafa was held up for a fortnight until fresh native gangs were drafted from Egypt.

Once again we bivouacked at Khan Yunis. The camels had a delightful time. Some of them broke loose, and finding their way into fields of young barley gorged themselves to such an extent that they developed pains in their interiors. We were unable to ride them for several days. We gorged ourselves on large and luscious oranges sold to us by the Arab women. They were surprised when we paid for them. They told us the Turks had also purchased large quantities of oranges and promised to pay for them—some other time.

Chapter 12

It seemed uncanny how the Turkish airmen were able to locate the exact whereabouts of large forces of troops and where we had guns concealed. One morning a Camel Corps patrol riding from Khan Yunis noticed a spiral of smoke rising in the air from a spot in the village where we had several guns. The patrol also noticed a Turkish plane hovering overhead. They became suspicious, but decided to say nothing just then. Two hours later the enemy taube came over and bombed the guns. Then it dawned upon the Camel patrol that the smoke spirals from Arab fires were signals to the Turks watching from above. That afternoon several Arabs were arrested in Khan Yunis, and one of them was found to be a Turk in disguise. Smoking fires were then forbidden, and we had fewer visits from taubes.

At Deir el Belah, where many of our mounted troops were camped, the Arabs used to worry the men for empty kerosene or biscuit tins, to be used, as they said, for carrying water. One morning a keen-eyed light horseman, scanning the sky for taubes, noticed one of these tins perched on top of a tall tree, close to which was a battery. Then seeing two other tins in nearby trees he spoke to his commanding officer about them. With the assistance of the sun's rays the tins were doing the work of a crude heliograph. The officer had the guns removed immediately. Barely were they under cover elsewhere when two taubes came over and bombed the vacated position. After that the Arabs got something more than tins when they came looking for them.

On the morning of 17 April, the second attack on Gaza began; it was to be the biggest battle, so far, in the history of Palestine. The troops participating immeasurably outnumbered any of the armies engaged in the countless campaigns which had taken place in the Holy Land. The Turks and Germans had been busy men since the first attack on 26 March. In twenty-four days Gaza had been turned into a modern fortress, and enemy reinforcements had been brought in thousands from the Caucasus, Mesopotamia, and Galicia. An important ridge east of Gaza had also been fortified to prevent our mounted troops from again encircling the town.

That night Mick Burke came across to our lines. Since transferring from his company I had seen little of him.

"Well, me noble hero," he said, squatting on his heels in front of my bivvy, "big things are going to happen in a day or so."

"What makes you think that?"

"Lots of things. Seeing you are an old stager at this business of trying to wipe Turks off the face of the earth, I'm surprised you haven't noticed what has been happening during the past few days."

"I've noticed nothing unusual."

"Well, let me tell you, son, that some very unusual things have been happening. For a start, those Gyppo labourers we last noticed toiling on the railhead at Rafa have been going like scalded cats, with the result that fourteen miles of broad-gauge line have been brought up to Deir el Belah well under a fortnight. Considering the country is all hills and hollows, that's a fairly creditable performance on their part. Now, if you care to take a little stroll about a mile to the east of where we are now enjoying each other's company, you'll find thousands of Tommy infantry moving forward under cover of darkness. They are as thick as fleas in an Arab's hut; and behind them are coming big guns."

"That looks as if there's something doing."

"You bet your sweet life it does. Dan Cooney came back to our company this morning. He was in Cairo getting over a bad spin with dysentery; and he says they are cleaning out the hospital. Unless a man is minus a leg or arm, or has half his head missing, his next stop, after leaving the gay city of beer and bints, is right here in the front line."

"That means a big scrap."

Burke grinned. "My luck it does. They want the beds for the wounded who will be taken into the wards of those hospitals within the next few days. Well, I must be going, my boy. Hope when I see you again you will be alive and kicking. If there's a big disturbance in the near future, keep your head down, and use your legs if the odds are against you."

The next afternoon we moved from Khan Yunis, and did not halt until we arrived at Abasan el Kebir shortly after midnight. Here we dismounted and rested for three hours. During the day there had been a heavy bombardment towards Gaza. Later we learned that the Tommy infantry had captured the outer defences of the town.

At 4 a.m. we crossed the Wady Ghuzze in the vicinity of Tel el Jemmi without any interference from the enemy, and reached the south of Dumbell Hill. There we parted from our camels, and moved out to the cover of a hill facing the Turkish redoubts. Here we considered we were safe. Near us were the East Anglian Division and a brigade of light horse. Toward Samson's Ridge we could hear the stutter of machine-gun fire, and to the east of Gaza British monitors, and a French battleship were shelling the town. Everything was strangely quiet in our sector; as we stretched ourselves on the side of the hill we smoked and joked with each other. Suddenly our chattering was interrupted by the whine of a shell which burst above us. When the smoke cleared away we saw that several of our men had been hit by the shrapnel pellets. Ray Webb had been shot in the temple, and died some days later.

The Bing Boys now opened on the Turkish redoubts. At the same time we advanced downhill in short rushes under very heavy rifle and machine-gun fire. Men were falling fast. Captain A. R. Norris, who had taken charge of our company after the death of Captain Rae, fell, shot through the foot, and almost at the same moment Doc Wright and Jack Condon were wounded. Most of the men reached a shallow wady in front, but I and two others were unable to advance through the terrific barrage of machine-gun fire. We flattened ourselves on the grass-carpeted ground until a lull gave us a chance to reach the wady.

Just then de Lancey Forth came walking across the open as unconcernedly as if he had been strolling along a city street. If ever a man bore a charmed life it was this daredevil officer. Seeing us drop on the ground, he walked across to where we were lying with our faces buried in the grass.

"Are you all right, boys?" he said.

Once he stood near us, it was the signal for the enemy machine-gunners to concentrate their fire on him. I doubt if there was an inch of ground around us that was not disturbed by their bullets, and it was a miracle we were not hit. We swore under our breath at de Lancey Forth for coming over to us, and drawing the enemy fire to the spot where we were concealed.

He stood there, swinging a short cane in his hand, but all the time those half-closed eyes of his were glancing to right and left where men were still racing across the open toward the wady where they knew they would be safe from the whining bullets.

"Seems a pity all this barley will be trampled and shot down before the day is over," said de Lancey Forth, kicking a clump of the green crop with his boot.

"Damn the flamin' barley," muttered the little sergeant lying beside me.

"What's that?" said de Lancey Forth.

" I said that if we stay here we'll be knocked rotten," growled the sergeant.

A shell came screeching through the air. We jumped to our feet and raced toward the wady. Reaching the bank, we threw ourselves over and fell in a heap on the sand below. All the wind was knocked out of me, and as I lay gasping I glanced along the wady.

A Camelier was lying on his back a few yards in front of me, his sightless blue eyes set and staring at the sky. Another was lying on his side nursing a foot, half of which had been shot away; the blood from it was soaking the ground.

I stood up and looked around toward the barley flat over which I had dashed a few seconds previously. I was wondering what had happened to de Lancey Forth. There he was, walking slowly toward the wady. Suddenly he clutched with one hand at his shoulder, and almost dropped to his knees.

"De Lancy's hit," yelled a Camelier.

A dozen men jumped to their feet, ready to dash back and bring him to safety, but the gallant officer again straightened himself, and, still swinging the cane, walked toward the wady. Leaping over the bank he was soon surrounded by several Cameliers.

"Are you hurt, sir?" asked an officer.

"Oh, just a scratch. But I fear those blighters over there have spoiled a brand new helmet."

He removed the helmet from his head and pointed to a hole in the top of it.

"That bullet scorched the hair on my head as it whizzed past," he said. Then flashing a glance to right and left, he pointed to the opposite side of the wady:

"Line that bank, men, but keep your heads down. We may have to advance again in a few moments."

Away to the left men were cheering. There was a tank rumbling over the uneven ground. During the past few weeks we had counted heavily on the tanks in this attack, and now here was one of them moving slowly towards the enemy's wire-fringed trenches. We also cheered in a feeble sort of way. Cameliers from the 1st Battalion were strung out behind the tank in an irregular column. They moved slowly forward, thinking as we did, no doubt, that once the tank reached the trenches in front the Turks would surrender.

Lieutenant-Colonel Langley was in charge of the 1st Battalion. No. 2 Company was led by Captain A. E. G. Campbell, and No. 3 Company on the right was in charge of Captain F. H. Naylor. No. 4 Company, between Naylor's men and our company, was led by Captain H. R. Denson. The 2nd Battalion did not go into action.

The tank reached the enemy's redoubts, tore through the wire, and dragged many of the posts cut of the ground. There was little cover for the men of the 1st Battalion as they advanced over the open ground. The Tommy infantry to the right of the Cameliers were getting over the ground as quickly as possible, so our men were forced to hurry to keep a straight and unbroken line. So far the casualties had been light, and there were few gaps in the lines of advancing Cameliers.

When the men in No. 2 Company were a little over a thousand yards from the redoubt which was their objective, the tank crossed between the Tommy infantry and the Cameliers. The Turks now turned every gun on to it that they could bring into action. Huge slugs clanged against the iron plates of the tank and ricochetted in every direction. But the tank still went on.

We now received the order to advance, and soon we were on open ground again, led by Lieutenant Davidson and under a hail of shrapnel and high explosive shells.

In front of the trenches we were charging, the enemy had placed several men, but as we came closer they ran back.

We were now well divided as we raced forward. Then a big shell burst to the rear of us. The man on my right spun round and dropped in a heap, and at the same moment something struck me on the back. My legs lost all feeling and down I went. As I lay I wondered if it was a wound that would give me a trip back to Aussie. However, my luck was out. Feeling came back into my legs, and I thought it safer to be moving. Slowly I rose to my feet, then raced after my comrades.

As we neared the trenches the Turks began to retire, and

at such close range we dropped many. One youthful Turk was shot in the leg; unable to race any farther, he faced us and stood with folded arms.

"Bayonet the cow," yelled a Camelier.

"No, give the poor devil a chance," cried another.

We raced past him, and he hobbled away to the rear. Another Turk, a mere youth, with his rifle clutched in his hand, struggled to a sitting position, then toppled sideways. A Camelier tore the rifle from his grip, gazed at him for a few seconds, then bent down and put a water-bottle to his lips.

"Poor wretch! Wants to live like the rest of us."

The water gave the wounded man strength and he sat up. The Camelier took a field-dressing from his tunic and proceeded to bandage a wound in the Turk's head. A few yards away a young Turkish officer, shot in the leg, watched the Camelier's work of mercy. Struggling painfully to his feet, he hobbled to the Australian, and patted him on the shoulder:

"Good."

"Good be damned." cried the Camelier. "Go and bury yourself. I'm busy."

The officer smiled and lit a cigarette, wondering, no doubt, if the Australian with the bloodshot eyes was really sane.

The tank, which had been doing splendid work, now stalled in deep sand, but again moved forward. The men inside seemed dazed; instead of going forward, they directed the machine in such a way that it moved along in front of the advancing Cameliers, so bringing a hail of shrapnel over the advancing men. Then the tank turned and again moved towards the redoubt, then the khaki-coloured yelling men reached the redoubt with one terrific rush.

Hit several times by enemy shells, the tank burst into flames. The Cameliers dropped in all directions until only thirty of our company were left; but this handful never faltered for a moment. Joined by some twenty Tommies from the infantry they rushed six hundred Turks, who fled. Forty prisoners were taken.

During the first rush to the redoubt Captain Naylor. of No. 3 Company, was shot in the leg. His men urged him to go back, but he refused. Yelling at those behind to follow him, he stumbled forward only to be killed as soon as he reached the redoubt. Lieutenants Allan, Wells, Matthews, Clark, and Young were wounded just about the time they arrived at the Turkish trenches.

Almost at the same time No. 11 and No. 12 Companies were also finding themselves in a tight corner in their attempt to capture Sheikh Abbas Ridge. The Turks now began to counter-attack. Our ranks were swept by bullets, and plastered with shells from guns of all calibres. Supports were unable to give us any assistance owing to the heavy artillery fire. The enemy machine-gunners now directed their fire on to the men in No. 12 Company who were concealed in a barley-field and using their Lewis guns when opportunity offered. Johnny Norton was shot through the chest. His inseparable pal, Alex Gibson, went to his assistance only to be shot down beside his mate. Another Camelier, named Gwider, who had got mixed up with our Lewis gunners while advancing over the open ground, was shot in the abdomen, and Vin Hennessy was hit in the leg, Bill McManus rolled over with a bullet through his arm, while Alf Kennett was shot through the mouth, and a bullet furrowed the top of Levy Tompkins's head. Only five of the Lewis gunners were now left.

Lieutenant-Colonel de Lancey Forth was still moving about the field; several times a bullet had pierced his uniform. The wound in his shoulder was troubling him, but he refused to leave his men. Seeing the desperate plight of No. 12 Company, he ordered Lieutenant Davidson to go to the light horsemen on our right, and ask them to hold their position until we retired, as the Turks had now almost encircled us.

With Lieutenant Kinkead and Sergeant Wilkie, I was stretched out on a grassy knob. From this lofty point we had a fine view of what was happening in the trenches so gallantly taken by the handful of English infantry and Australian Cameliers on our left. They had now held the captured trench for two hours, and during that time had repulsed every Turkish attack. Their remarkable stand was the most heroic incident in our second attack on Gaza. A week later English newspapers claimed that every one of these men should have received the V.C.

We saw a German officer, minus his tunic, and with his shirt-sleeves rolled up, jump on top of the main Turkish redoubt and beckon the men below to follow him in a charge towards our positions. The Turks refused.

That German officer was a brave man. Scores of our men tried to bring him down, but all failed. He seemed to bear a charmed life.

Seeing that all of his men were likely to be shot down, Captain Campbell sent six runners with messages for assistance: four were killed; the others wounded. At last he ordered the few remaining men to retire to a narrow wady a short distance to the right. He then went to his Lewis gunners: five were dead beside their guns; the sixth, a man named Barry, had his arm shattered.

The officer ordered Barry to save himself as best he could. He asked what he would do with his gun. Campbell told him to leave it and get away as quickly as possible. Barry refused to do this, and carried the gun away with him.

Another hero of this small band of survivors was Quartermaster-Sergeant (later Lieutenant) H. L. D. Malcolm, whose place was at the rear. He had joined in the attack on the Turkish redoubts "just for the fun of it," as he said later. He moved among the wounded men, dressing their injuries and giving them water to drink. When not doing this he used a rifle he had picked up, and shot several Turks. When he and Lieutenant E. J. Aylwin were the only two Australians left, Campbell ordered Malcolm to lead the way to the rear.

"I'll be damned if I will," said Malcolm.

Lieutenant Aylwin then dashed away, followed by Campbell and Malcolm. Aylwin was hit by several bullets as he ran, but managed to get back safely. Campbell did not receive a scratch. He was one of only five men of the hundred in his company who did not become casualties during those terrible hours on the summit of Tank Redoubt—as this spot was afterwards named.

Half a dozen Cameliers had been taken prisoners. A German officer ordered them to the rear where they were given water to drink. Two of the Cameliers, Bert Storey and Kelly, had no intention of being held as prisoners, so they leaped the parapet and ran towards the Wady Ghuzze. Strange to say, despite Turkish riflemen and machine-gunners, they reached the wady uninjured, although Kelly afterwards showed a couple of bullet-holes in his hat.

While the light horsemen were advancing on our right their horses remained in the wady, where they were noticed by the enemy airmen. Soon afterwards a storm of shell from the enemy's heavy guns broke over the horses; but the men holding the animals moved up and down the gully as the Turkish shelling necessitated— in fact, these horse-holders tired out the guns by their splendid discipline and cool courage.

The Bing Boys, who had ably supported us during the morning, came in for a very bad shelling. One of their guns was dismantled by a direct hit, and all its crew were wounded, but the remainder stuck to their guns with magnificent coolness. At last they were forced to retire. As they passed several Cameliers, one of them said in a plaintive voice:

"We finish, Johnnie."

Several men of No. 12 Company, during their advance, crossed the Beersheba Road, and occupied a grassy rise beyond it, where they were joined by a squadron of the 11th Light Horse. These men had also advanced over the open ground under continual showers of shrapnel and high-explosive shells. General Headquarters doubted the claim that No. 12 Company had penetrated such a distance. When the ground was cleared of Turks eight months later, the dead bodies of three Cameliers were found where they fell, well past the Beersheba Road.

Although Lieutenant Davidson displayed great bravery in delivering de Lancey Forth's message to the 11th Light Horse to stand their ground while the Cameliers retired, the Australian horsemen had their own orders, so No. 12 Company was left to get on the best way it could. Seeing it was madness to advance any farther, our O.C. now gave the order to withdraw. Almost at the same moment the light horsemen also began to fall back.

It was a stubborn, angry withdrawal. Hundreds of Cameliers had been put out of action in trying to capture the Turkish redoubts, and their mates hated to go back after such a sacrifice. Reluctantly they went back, stopping every few seconds to turn on the enemy who were slowly following them.

A sturdy young Camelier with a hand stained with the blood from a wound in his shoulder, raised and shook it at the advancing Turks:

"By the living God, we'll shift you next time!"

While retreating, Lewis gunners Byers and Walker met a Turk we had missed while advancing. Apparently he was a sniper who had continued to fire at our men after they had passed. The two ordered him to go back with them, but seeing the Turks advancing, he refused to do so. Walker drew his revolver and shot him dead.

Chapter 13

As we straggled back to the wady we had crossed in the morning, the enemy guns opened up a devastating fire, and we sought shelter in the many sandy gullies branching from the main wady. I rushed towards a steep rise where a light horse officer was standing alone, giving orders. When I reached the base of the rise, the screech of a shell sent me racing up a nearby gully; then I turned and saw the shell burst on the summit of the rise. When the dust cleared the officer was gone.

I continued along the gully, and a few minutes later came to a Tommy lying against the steep bank. He was only a boy, and a sickly grin spread over his face as I approached.

"Hullo, what are you doing here?"

"I was hit with shrapnel in the infantry charge this morning. I would like you to see where I am wounded. I am not feeling too good—I wish I had a drink of water."

"But why didn't you wait until stretcher-bearers picked you up?"

"There were others worse who wanted attending to, so I crawled up here to wait until the fight was over."

I bent over him and he pointed to the lower part of his tunic. Removing it and lifting his shirt, I saw a two-inch V-shaped gash, beneath which the intestines showed.

"Do you think that will get me to Blighty?" asked the Tommy, putting a match to the cigarette I had handed him.

I felt like telling him he would be lucky if the wound did not take him on a longer journey than to England. The jagged cut was already septic.

"Hop on my back and I'll take you to a dressing-station."

"I've got another wound." Here he held out his left foot, which had been concealed by a partly unwound putty. Portion of his heel had been shot away.

"Come on. There's no time to waste with you, me lad, or you'll never see Blighty again."

He managed to clamber on my back, and slowly I moved along the floor of the narrow wady. Turning a corner, I came to half a dozen Bing Boys seated in a group. They did not speak. By the look of their eyes they had been crying. Those splendid men had lost several old friends that morning, and the frightful shelling of their position by the enemy guns had shattered the nerves of the survivors.

There was a fantass of water near where they were seated. I asked one of them to let me have a drink for the wounded man on my back. A big bearded Indian slowly raised his head. I think he had been asleep.

"Camel Corps, Johnnie?" he asked, pointing to the wounded man.

"No, infantry."

The Indian pointed to the fantass. "Not much water, Johnnie. Might get little bit."

I lowered the Tommy to the ground and gave him a drink of the muddy water. He did not speak, and I could see he was in a bad way. Once again I hoisted him on my back. A short distance ahead was Dumbell Hill, where there was an infantry dressing-station. As I moved away I turned to one of the Bing Boys.

"Many of your men killed!"

"All finish, Johnnie. All finish!" And his voice ended in a big sob.

It was tiring work carrying the wounded man; slowly I moved along the wady. Then there came a rumbling noise, and before I had time to crouch against the side of the wady, a big shell burst on the bank. I was thrown several yards away, and portion of the bank fell on top of me. The Tommy lay where I had dropped him.

Somewhat dazed, I scooped the dirt out of my mouth and eyes. Blood was trickling down my face from where a fragment of shell had scratched my forehead. The Tommy had fared better than myself. There was a grin on his face as he crawled over to where I was lying. I cannot say how long we stayed there, but seeing our plight from Dumbell Hill, two men with a stretcher came hurrying towards us. They placed the Tommy on the stretcher, then one of them had a look at me.

"Take off your tunic," he said, "and have a look at it."

I did so and found that the band at the back had been cut away; and there was a ragged rent on the back of the flannel I was wearing. A vivid red mark showed on the flesh. I remembered the shell that had burst near me earlier in the day, and the soreness of my back for some time afterwards. Another fraction of an inch and the piece of shell would have fractured my spine.

Wishing the Tommy on the stretcher all sorts of luck, I wandered over the hill and came to the spot where we had left our camels early in the morning. Some of the men in my company had already returned and were sprawled out on the grass. I poured some water into the crown of my hat and washed my face. Just then a Gyppo passed us leading a camel with two cacolets swaying on its back. The hood was slowly lifted on one of the cacolets, and a grinning face gazed at me. It was Snowy Allen.

"Give me a cigarette. I stopped a lump of ironmongery, and me liver feels as if it's been knocked through me kidneys."

He got the cigarette and the camel moved on.

A few minutes later Major Donovan ordered us to mount our camels, and lead to the men who were still in the wady, their animals. Later there was much comment about this incident. No doubt the officer thought that by taking the camels towards the wady, the men there would be able to mount them and ride back to a spot where they could rest.

We rode over the rise and down the other side until we came to a hollow. Then the first shell came, followed by others. The

Turks could not resist turning their guns on such a conspicuous target. We should have turned and hurried back; instead, we barraked the animals and crouched down beside them. It was a miracle that every man and camel was not killed. Shells burst over us in rapid succession. Camels were hit and the blankets piled on top of the saddles burst into flames.

Tommy infantry lined the summit of Dumbell Hill, and they kept calling out:

"Run! you silly blighters. Run!"

One man took their advice. Jumping up from be side his camel, he raced towards the Tommies. He had only covered half the distance when a shell got him and he lay in a huddled heap.

We crouched closer to the camels, but despite this living barricade, three men were killed and others wounded.

"This is damned murder!" cried a Camelier. "Let us move back in a body or we will all be killed."

Jerking the camels to their feet, and leading those that were able to walk, we raced toward the ridge we had crossed a short time previously. Several dead Cameliers and many dead and wounded animals were left behind. Strange to say, the enemy gunners did not fire at us as we retired. Soon we reached a place of safety where, later, the Cameliers from the wady joined us.

After their retirement at midday these men had lined the wady and remained there all afternoon, the Scotties with their Vickers guns preventing the Turks from advancing. On the opposite side of the wady the Tommy infantry lay in support. At dusk the Cameliers retired another three hundred yards, where they dug in with their bayonets. During the early part of the night the Turks fired spasmodically, and judging by the Very lights they sent up at intervals, they were panicky. About a hundred and fifty yards separated their outposts from the Cameliers; and German officers in their lines taunted.

"I thought the Australians never ran," came a voice from the darkness.

We had been warned not to reply. But many of the exhausted Cameliers would have welcomed the order to again race across the open with fixed bayonets and settle accounts with those jeering Germans.

At 9 p.m. de Lancey Forth, who, despite his wound, still refused to leave his men, assembled the remnants of each company and marched them back to where we were waiting with the camels. After a hasty meal we replenished rations, water, and ammunition, but were ordered not to go to sleep.

At three the following morning we went forward on foot towards Dumbell Hill, where we dug in. Many men went to sleep, and the officers were unable to arouse them.

I was one of a party detailed to assist Tommy engineers to erect barbed-wire entanglements between our lines and those held by the enemy. Each carrying an iron peg and rifle, we wandered in the darkness but could not locate the Tommies. After a time we heard low voices coming from behind a clump of bushes some distance away. Dropping the iron pegs, we sprawled full length on the ground, then crawled inch by inch toward the bushes. When only a few yards from them we could distinguish three Turks lying on the grass. There was a sudden rush, some smart bayonet work, and we retired quickly to our lines leaving three dead Turks behind the bushes. We made no further effort to find the engineers, but fell asleep in a half-burrowed trench.

Day was breaking when we were aroused by a taube droning overhead. It swooped low down over our trenches, then flew back to the enemy lines, despite our rifle-fire. The taube returned half an hour later and dropped three bombs on the infantry who were digging trenches on our right. One killed six Tommies outright, and wounded many others.

During the day we extended our trenches along the summit of the ridge, enemy airmen taking a keen interest in what we were doing. Evidently, they were trying to locate the whereabouts of the guns manned by the Bing Boys and Tommies, which were concealed at the rear of our trenches. The Indians were using their guns to keep the taubes at a distance. Every time one of the planes hovered over their place of concealment they threw overcoats over their guns and then lay low. Late in the afternoon there was much activity in the enemy lines. We prepared for an attack, but our guns played such havoc in their ranks that they apparently thought it wiser to remain where they were.

Night brought a cold wind from the sea; we shivered in our trenches. Want of sleep was beginning to play strange pranks with us; there were times when we imagined we could see large bodies of men charging us over the open ground. Two Cameliers started to fight because one asked the other if he would like someone to present him with a kapok mattress, so that he could go to sleep. Almost any jest referring to sleep would have started a fight during those trying hours.

One man did not sleep. Padre Little, of the Camel Corps, was always on the move. From the time we first went into action he had unceasingly attended to the wounded and the dying. Many a dying man smiled happily as the last breath flickered from his body, owing to the presence of this noble man by his side, and the soft prayers that he uttered.

When the six Tommies were killed by an aerial bomb earlier in the morning our padre hastened to where their mangled bodies were. Bending over them, he seemed to be busy for quite a long time. When he came back we asked him what he had been doing.

"Preparing those poor boys for burial. Their arms end legs were lying everywhere, so I just gave them their missing limbs. Their relatives at home would not like to think they had been buried without them."

Those reckless, devil-may-care Cameliers felt they were very close to God when Padre Little was with them.

Under cover of darkness camels came up behind our trenches with rations and blankets. There was a mix-up in distributing them. Some men got blankets, while others only received rations.

One irate Camelier went over to Lieutenant "Jock" Davidson with a blanket in his hand:

"How the blazes am I going to eat this?"

"Make a stew of it."

The Camelier retired mumbling, but half an hour later he was found asleep in a side trench with the blanket wrapped round him. And someone had put a couple of tins of bully-beef under his head for a pillow.

Early the following morning the trenches were left lightly manned, while most of us retired to a nearby wady, and there slept all day. At night we went back to the trenches; but early next day we were relieved by the infantry and rode back to Khan Yunis. The village was shining like an emerald as we came back to it, dust-stained and weary. We were exceedingly grateful for the change. We camped near the cactus hedges which afforded admirable protection from observation by enemy aircraft which still hovered in the neighbourhood.

The first Sunday morning we all attended church parade. Padre Little referred to our heavy casualties, and to the pals we had all lost. Then he asked the solemn-faced Cameliers if there was a man amongst them who, during the long hours they faced the Turks at Gaza, had not offered up a prayer for himself or comrade. He asked the men who had not done so to put up their hands. There was no response.

On the outskirts of the meeting stood Brigadier-General Smith, V.C., G.O.C. of the Imperial Camel Corps There were tears in the hero's eyes. The previous day one of our officers spoke to him and referred to our heavy casualties. With a sob in his voice, the General said:

"I'll never be able to replace those men. He walked away, and spoke to no man for two days.

Chapter 14

On 19 May we mounted our camels, and with many grunts and gurgles the soft-footed animals trotted away in the direction of Rafa. That ride was one of the worst we had experienced. A dust-storm worked up during the afternoon, and now clouds of sand were sweeping over the open ground—sand that struck exposed flesh like a whip-lash, and cut the skin so that pencil-lines of blood came. We rode with bowed heads and hats pulled down to shield the eyes. Those of us who had handkerchiefs tied them over nose and mouth. However, our hearts were light as we believed we were going to rest here, at Rafa, on the shores of the Mediterranean for many weeks. There would be swimming and long hours of sleep undisturbed by nightly patrols. We even looked forward to Cairo leave.

That showed how much we knew. A few days later we were issued with full rations and ammunition; we even had a rifle inspection. The rumour went round that another attempt was to be made to take Gaza. It was not a cheering outlook. We would be wiped out altogether.

"That's the way they do things," growled a Camelier. "When they get good fighting men they keep pushing them into the front line until they are all wiped out. Look at me. I'm gone in the hind-legs now, and if I go into another scrap the next thing I'll know is that I am presenting arms before old Peter at the Pearly Gates."

"Yes," said another, "and if a fellow goes on sick parade, and says he's crook, the M.O. will grin at him and say, 'By gad! What do you think of that, now? Here's one of those hardy Cameliers who thinks there's something wrong with him. Give the poor fellow a dose of whitehouse.' Yes, whitehouse. No matter what's wrong with you, that's the stuff they reckon will fix you up."

We left Rafa after dark, but before we had gone far we could see that Gaza was not our destination. Then word flitted along the line that the Cameliers were to assist in a big raid on one of the Turkish lines of communication. Major-General Chauvel was in charge of operations, and to make a success of this little job he selected the cavalry, light horse, and Cameliers to assist him.

South-east of Beersheba lies El Auja, and south of that desert outpost is another called Maan. The latter is on the main line of the Hejaz Railway from Medina to Damascus. In spite of their retreat toward Gaza the Turks still clung to this line, and kept large forces at each of the outposts. These troops were a constant menace to our right flank. The strongest outpost was at Maan. From that garrison troops could easily be sent via El Auja to Beersheba if they were needed. Therefore the object of our raid was to destroy a large section of the railway between Beersheba and El Auja.

Throughout the night we rode slowly with no more than an occasional halt for a few minutes. Just as dawn was breaking we reached the Wady el Abiad and dismounted for breakfast. We were not sorry of this chance to stretch our legs. It was a dull, wearisome business sitting on the back of a camel all night. Here the country was rugged with barren, rocky hills on both sides of us—a land entirely devoid of vegetation.

We had part of a light horse regiment with us, and they dismounted close to where we had halted. Jimmy Moore rode across to see if he knew any of them.

"Take that stinking brute of yours away from here," said a tall, lean light horseman. "Our horses might object to the smell of it, and if they stampede we'll be lucky to stop them before they get back to Australia."

Moore was tired and sleepy, and perhaps the monotonous surroundings had put an edge to his temper.

"Yes," he snapped back, "you blokes object to our stinking camels, but, by cripes, you're glad to have us with you when there's a scrap on."

"Oh, go and lose yourself."

"Lose myself, did you say?" yelled Moore. "Yes, you're a great mob, you are, riding about like blanky earls while we have to work like niggers."

The light horseman slowly filled his pipe, at the same time keeping one eye on the irate Camelier. The other troopers sprawled about the sand were enjoying the exchange of compliments.

"You're a grateful sort of coot, you are," added the light horseman, "considering you have to take the blanky light horse with you everywhere you go to stop the bloomin' lousy Arabs from running away with you."

Moore's rejoinder was lost in the laughter that followed; and the Cameliers joined in the mirth.

Once again in the saddle, we rode towards El Auja. When we reached it the garrison was retiring in the distance. Had it not been for the halt at the Wady el Abiad we would have secured a nice haul of prisoners. We found the outpost deserted; our aeroplanes had played havoc with the buildings.

El Auja was the best laid out garrison we had visited since we started on the big advance from the Canal. In the centre of the settlement there was a beautiful park with statues, and bordered by Australian gum-trees. Closer examination revealed that underneath this park were tunnels into which the garrison retired at the approach of our bombing planes.

As we approached El Auja the light horse and cavalry made a demonstration against Beersheba, and drove back the Turkish mounted troops, while the artillery shelled their defences. One of our planes reconnoitred and reported by a note dropped in a parachute that a big viaduct could easily be destroyed. A sixty-pounder was brought on the scene and laid it in ruins, then dropped several shells on a Turkish train farther down the line. Stone bridges and culverts were blown up, and rails scattered over the surrounding country. For more than an hour there was a continuous roar of detonations; we could see huge clouds of smoke and dirt soaring into the air in the distance. Thus ended the Turkish menace from the south; the damage done by our demolition parties was a severe blow to them.

As there was nothing more for us to do thereabouts, we started back just before sunset. A few miles from El Auja, Arabs or Turks sniped us from a rocky hill on our left. It was long-range shooting and did no damage. At the Wady el Abiad we bivouacked. Here one of our aeroplanes, while trying to land, had bent an axle and damaged other minor parts. The pilot, being unable to repair the damage without a forge and the necessary tools, was seriously thinking of destroying the machine to prevent it falling into the hands of the enemy.

Two Cameliers strolled across and inspected the damaged machine, scratched their heads, examined it again, then casually told the pilot they reckoned they could fix it. The pilot laughed, but told them to get busy if they wished to do so. They went for a walk and returned with part of an iron rail (that had been hurled into the air during the demolition stunt earlier in the day) and some telegraph wire. Making a fire, and using the rail for an anvil, they heated and straightened the axle; wrapped wire round other damaged parts; then informed the pilot he could hop into his bus and fly away. The pilot stepped into the machine, waved to the Cameliers, and was off like a bird.

Next day we met several Bedouin shepherds guarding some thirty sheep. The Cameliers offered to buy the animals, holding out money. The Bedouins disdainfully refused. Then several Cameliers jumped to the ground and proceeded to butcher the sheep and divide the mutton amongst their mates. Appeals from officers to cease the slaughter fell on deaf ears. The men were heartily sick and tired of bully-beef, and could not resist the chance of getting fresh mutton when it was there for the taking. At Rafa that night savoury odours drifted from the lines where we bivouacked; and when the juicy chops were distributed the officers received their share. They, also, detested bully-beef, and although they declared they did not approve of the way the sheep had been taken, they enjoyed the cooked mutton.

We had finished supper and were preparing for a good night's sleep when we were ordered to saddle up and move towards Gaza. That annoyed the Cameliers; they mumbled, grumbled, and swore at each other and at everything. Jimmy Moore expressed his opinions rather forcibly to Sergeant Wilkie:

"Here's us dog-tired after riding for three days and nights with only a few hours' sleep between, and now, just when we're ready to turn into our blankets, we've got to move again. I ask you, fair and square, as man to man, are the Camel Corps the only blanky troops on this front?"

"Looks like it. But, if you promise not to repeat it, I'll tell you something."

Moore dropped the durra bag he was about to place on the side of his saddle:

"I won't whisper a dashed word of anything you tell me."

"Well, the first hundred years of this sort of thing are the worst; after that, you'll find the going dead easy."

"Bah!" grunted Moore, hoisting the durra bag on the saddle. A few seconds later a long line of grunting and snorting camels stepped slowly over the sand.

It was another nightmare ride. Although we had rested at Wady el Abiad the previous night, few of the men had closed their eyes. We were too tired to sleep. The last five miles of that night ride from Rafa were the hardest I ever remember. Men and camels were worn out. Two hours after midnight we were ordered to dismount and rest for an hour. We just threw ourselves down and slept, only to be aroused a few seconds later (so it seemed) and ordered to mount again. We moved off half asleep.

A light breeze fanned our faces as dawn broke, and we

gazed with heavy eyes at a patch of scarlet ahead: it was a field of poppies. The camels tramped them under their padded feet. Then more sand—and ahead of us was the Wady Ghuzze. Everything was quiet; if there was a war the troops on both sides seemed to be concealing the fact.

We passed Sheikh Nuran, and five miles to the southwest again threw ourselves down on the sand to sleep. An enemy plane came and hovered for a few seconds overhead. A dozen bombs could fall from it for all we cared. But the machine passed and we slumbered.

Chapter 15

After many blessed hours of sleep we were ordered to make a permanent camp. The unit was to remain here for some time, provided Abdul did not take it into his head to push us back. Evidently he was not feeling like further fighting just then, so we were not disturbed for several days. We erected bivvies and dug funk-holes into which we dropped when a taube flew overhead. Lying on our backs in these narrow pits we would watch the black speck high overhead until the droning of a descending bomb convinced every man in every hole that it was going to drop right into the pit where he was sheltering. Then there would be a deafening crash, perhaps a quarter of a mile away. We would jump from the funk-holes, rub the dirt out of our eyes, and ask each other: "Where did that one drop?"

The Bing Boys, bivouacked near our lines, enjoyed the coming of these taubes, as it gave them an opportunity to test their guns for aerial work. I cannot remember ever seeing the Indians drop an enemy plane, but their shells occasionally burst so close to them that those in the machines thought it wiser to drop their "eggs" somewhere else. For several days the Bing Boys had things all their own way, as it were—they were doing all the shelling without the enemy aviators hitting back. It gave the Indians confidence, and they became quite cheeky until one morning a taube came over and dropped a couple of bombs amongst them. None of them were injured, but one of their guns resembled a heap of scrap iron. After that the Bing Boys treated the taubes with greater respect, and only fired at them when they had passed the spot where the guns were concealed.

There was a shortage of wood among us, so it was not long before a couple of deserted Bedouin huts on the other side of the wady attracted our attention. The walls were made from straw bricks, but the rafters were wood. Enemy snipers had the huts covered; but that did not prevent the Cameliers dashing from the wady and racing over open ground until they came to the shacks. Here, sheltered by the walls, we would pull down portion of the roof, and when the cloud of dust that followed the descending timber had cleared away we would select what we wanted and race back to the wady.

Those huts were infested with fleas, and before we could get away from them our arms and legs would be covered with the lively little insects. Once we reached the wady we would drop the wood, remove our clothing, and proceed to exterminate those fleas that did not have the sense to hop into the surrounding sand. Tommies bivouacked near Tel el Jemmi derived much amusement from our antics, but we could see nothing funny in it.

One morning after we had raided the huts and were jumping about on the sandy bed of the wady, as naked as the day we were born, a couple of Tommy artillery officers strolled over towards us.

"By Jove," one of them drawled, "I never saw such extraordinary dancing in my life. Tell me, men, is that a native dance you do back in Australia?"

Big Jack Condon glared at the speaker:

"Yes. It's a blanky dance we do when we are pestered by inquisitive cows who ask damn-fool questions."

The officer grinned. "I'm astonished. Such graceful movements by burly men like yourselves is something that will linger in my mind for quite a long time."

Laughing, the two officers went back to Tel el Jemmi, and Condon glared at them as they walked away.

"You know," he said, after a long pause, "there's times when I feel like getting down on my marrowbones and praying to the Lord for promotion to the rank of an officer so that I could meet funny blokes like that cove on an equal footing. By cripes, I'd fix 'em! I'd------"

Here a flea nipped the back of his neck and he did not finish the sentence.

One of the reinforcements sent to fill the gaps in our ranks after the second Gaza battle was a lad named Spinks; I believe he enlisted in Sydney. I mention this owing to the fact that on my return to Australia I had a message for his parents—the last words of a dying son—but I could not trace their whereabouts. This boy (barely eighteen years old) came to us one afternoon after rations had been drawn for the next twenty-four hours, so he looked like going without anything to eat until rations were drawn for him the following day. At this time we drew rations for groups of four men, and unless one of the group happened to be away, there was no food to spare. I spoke to the three men in my group, and we decided to take Spinks in with us until the following day. The lad seemed grateful. He had a frightened look in his eyes, which was nothing unusual, as most of these boyish reinforcements were a wee bit scared when they learned what had happened to the Cameliers during the second attack on Gaza.

The following morning we were ordered to take all sick camels on our lines to brigade headquarters, a quarter of a mile away. I was one of those detailed for the job. But I happened to be scraping a two weeks' growth of hair from my face at the time, so Spinks offered to take my place. I picked out half a dozen of the camels, and he led them away while I went on with my shaving.

A few minutes later we heard the buzzing noise of a taube in the distance, and soon the machine was hovering over our lines. Then came the whine of a falling bomb, and we raced for our funk-holes. It exploded with a shattering roar near the latrines between our lines and brigade headquarters. Two more followed. When the dust had cleared we could see dead and wounded men and camels lying on the ground.

We raced across to the scene of destruction. Most of the sick camels taken from our lines were dead or wounded. The first wounded man I came across was Spinks. Bending over him, I could see he was in a bad way. Getting a stretcher, another Camelier and I hurried with him to the dressing-station at the rear of headquarters. We had not gone far before he muttered feebly for us to halt. We could see he was dying. He was game to the last. A few whispered words, another smile, and a plucky little warrior had gone to meet his Maker.

Since I first stepped on the sandy beach at Anzac I had watched many men die, but the passing of none of them lingered longer in my mind than the sudden death of poor little Spinks. If I had not been shaving when the order came to remove the sick camels from our lines he would not have got in the way of the falling bombs. Somehow, I felt responsible for his death. But my stretcher mate, Frank Matzonas, would not listen to me:

"That's not right. If a fellow's time has come to go, he's got to go, and nothing will save him."

I cannot say how many men were killed as a result of the bombs dropped from the taube that morning. Several were carried away with ghastly wounds only to die days later. The orderly room sergeant lay outside his tent, and his death must have been instantaneous ; others were lying dead at the latrines; a lump of flying iron had overtaken another man as he raced across a flat from headquarters. When we picked him up portion of his head was missing.

Forty-two camels were stretched out dead at the spot where they had been assembled a few minutes previously. Many others were wounded, and some of them had to be destroyed. The Cameliers were detailed for one of the worst digging jobs we had yet experienced. With picks and shovels we started to dig huge trenches to put the dead camels in. We worked all day. Never before was such growling and grumbling heard amongst the men of the Camel Corps. They reckoned it was bad enough to dig miles of trenches that might never be used, but it was over the odds digging graves for dead camels.

Not only did we dig these huge holes, but the dead camels had to be dragged into them. That was slow work. To make matters worse, the camels objected to dragging their dead mates; they would stop every few yards, curl their lips, gurgle in their queer way, then flop down on the sand. Sometimes the liberal use of an army boot made them alter their minds, and after much more gurgling and grunting, they would get on with the job.

Late that night the last camel was buried. Outside my bivvy I found Mick Burke awaiting my return. I had not seen him since the second Gaza stunt, but men in his company had told me he came out of the engagement without a scratch.

"That Hun airman gave you a full issue this morning," he said, "and I came across to see if you were alive and kicking."

"Looks as if I'm still alive. But being a blanky undertaker for dead camels doesn't agree with me. I'm that dashed tired I could lie down and sleep for a week."

"Better not do it. There might be another taube over in the morning, and you don't want to be asleep if the bloke in it chucks more explosives overboard."

"Don't they bomb your crowd?"

Mick grinned. "My oath they do. One of them frightened six months' growth out of me yesterday. I was one of a patrol prowling about over Beersheba way. Over came a taube and bombed us. When the bombs ran out the fellow in the plane turned his blanky machine-gun on us until his bullets finished, then he fired his revolver at us until it was empty. Noticing me racing over open ground on my camel, he came lower still and threw a blanky spanner at me."

"Cripes! He meant to get you," said Jimmy Moore, who had sauntered across to my bivvy. "Reminds me of the taube that chased Darkie Fox the other day. He must have had only one bomb on board, and he presented it to Darkie—from the air, of course. The noise it made in falling so put the wind up Darkie that when it exploded many yards away he fell off his camel, and the stupid animal bolted towards the horizon. The airman came down lower to see what damage he had done, and Darkie, thinking he was going to open up with his machine-gun, pulled off his tunic and put up his fists:

"'Come on, you purple cow, and fight me fair,' he roared."

"I'll bet that tickled the Hun," said Mick. "If he happened to be Lieutenant Felmy I'll wager he has told all the enemy airmen, and they are laughing about it between here and Constantinople."

"Felmy wouldn't do a thing like that," remarked Moore. "He's the most chivalrous adversary we've had anything to do with since we left the Canal. Look at what he did a few weeks back. He dropped two of our machines, then sent a letter to No. 1 Squadron by another plane stating that one of our officers had been killed, and that another named Vautin was well but wanted his kit. Soon afterwards Major Murray Jones flew across to the enemy lines with Vautin's clothing and mail from Australia. Jones descended to within fifty feet over the German aerodrome and dropped the parcel among the officers waiting there, returning their hand-waving as he circled the ground. That's what I call playing the game. When men in armies opposed to each other do that sort of thing it makes a fellow believe war isn't such a rotten business after all."

Burke agreed. " Felmy's a sport, all right. He was in the plane that hovered over our headquarters soon after the last Gaza stunt, and dropped a bag with letters from Camelier prisoners, also a list of our men who had been killed in their trenches. You can always tell Felmy's machine. It is a black-tailed taube. And by cripes, when I spot it hovering over our lines, you can't see me for dust."

There were other things besides aerial bombs that annoyed us in this camp near the Wady Ghuzze. To secure protection from bomb splinters and to increase the dimensions of our bivvies, we dug holes about three feet in depth and put bivouac sheets over the cavities. We rarely removed any clothes at night (excepting boots or putties) when we turned into our bivvies. It was then that the scarab beetle got busy. He was an energetic sort of insect who selected his dinner at the camel-lines, and returned with it until he found one of our bivvies in his way. Then the scarab and his foul-smelling load fell on top of us. Sometimes the curses of an angry Camelier disturbed the stillness of the night when he awoke to find a couple of large beetles inside his trousers. Many devices were tried to deal with this nuisance; the most effective was a trench around the bivvy. The flat of a shovel kept the scarab population down, but there were always a few left to disturb our slumbers at night.

Chapter 16

Towards the end of June the Cameliers told anyone who cared to listen that they were just about "fed up" with everything. Day after day we rode out to patrol the same stretches of country with the stunted bushes and sand-dunes. To break the monotony we would have welcomed a brush with the enemy; but even excitement like this was denied us. The yeomanry, New Zealanders, and Australian light horse occasionally sighted a Turkish mounted patrol and chased them back to the enemy lines. But we never got within miles of them. When not doing patrol work we remained in camp to remove ticks from camels, or apply mange dressing to their festering hides. This was a smellful business and, naturally, we did not like it.

Then we got camel itch, and scratched our flesh till sores came. There were nights when we scarcely closed our eyes—just lay and scratched. We had just about cured ourselves of this distressing complaint, when Alex Hislop contracted meningitis and died. Our camp was removed a mile away, and we were isolated from the other companies.

One morning we rode across to the rail-head at Deir el Belah, and there were ordered to undress. Then our clothing was placed in a closed railway truck to be fumigated. Meanwhile, we were allowed to wear our boots, and in them passed away time strolling around the food-dump or playing two-up. When those in charge of the fumigating train thought the "chats" were well and truly cooked, the steaming garments were handed back to us; then we dressed ourselves and returned to our lines.

At the end of June Sir Edmund Allenby arrived in Palestine to take over the duties of commander-in-chief. Somehow his presence cheered our drooping spirits. He came with a fine reputation, and we looked to him to do big things around Gaza in the near future. He visited all units, including the Cameliers, and an absence of "swank" convinced the fighting men that they "would get on pretty well with him." Soon after his arrival there was a notable increase in the quantity and quality of our rations; we were even issued with bottled beer. We didn't get much of it—one bottle to two men. Still, it was beer. General Allenby may not have been responsible for having it issued, but to us he got the credit for it.

Allenby had a habit of mingling amongst groups of men who were not aware of his presence in their midst; in this way he secured first-hand information concerning their complaints and opinions of things in general. One night Mick Burke, Jimmy Moore, and a few other Cameliers were discussing what should be done if the next attack on Gaza was to be a success.

"I'll tell you what I would do if I was Allenby," said Jimmy Moore. "I'd bring up about a million guns and a couple of thousand aeroplanes, and while the guns got to them in front the blanky planes could pelt them with bombs in the rear. After that our mounted men and infantry could tear into them, and before they would know what had happened, the Turks and their German cobbers, who were still alive, would be on their way as prisoners to Cairo."

Mick Burke did not agree. "You leave this little job to Allenby. When he's ready he'll put the kybosh on those fellows in front of us."

"Well, I hope he does. But I'd like to have a few minutes' talk with him. I'd give him some wrinkles that would show him how we could be in Jerusalem within a month."

There came a laugh out of the darkness behind the men and someone walked towards the officers' tents. Soon afterwards Sergeant Wilkie strolled across to us.

"What were you fellows talking about just now?" he said.

"Oh, Jimmy Moore was just telling us how Allenby ought to take Gaza," replied one of the Cameliers.

"You silly galoots," snorted the sergeant. "That was Allenby who just left here, and he heard every word you said."

The 1st Battalion of the Camel Corps now went back to the Suez Canal for a rest. We all agreed they were entitled to it after their heroic fighting and heavy casualties during the second attack on Gaza. The 4th Battalion, who had been roaming around Sinai for many months, took their place in the front line. Soon afterwards the O.C. of the 4th Battalion returned to Australia, and Lieutenant-Colonel Mills was placed in command of the unit. The Cameliers took an instant liking to their new leader. There was something about him that convinced them he would be well in the lead of their battalion when any fighting was to be done.

The main topic of conversation now was: When would Allenby start his big push! We all knew it was coming, and so did the Turk, but he could not guess at what point the British would attack. It was obvious to us that the third attack on Gaza would be made on the eastern flank. Night after night long lines of infantry marched from the Canal. Amongst them was an Irish division, which had a frightful time during the Serbian retreat in 1915, and after them came the 60th (London) Division. They had spent months at Salonika, after fighting in France and Macedonia. Grim-faced, sturdy men were these Tommies, and the Australians and New Zealanders liked the look of them.

Our right flank now became a scene of intense activity. One night a number of Indian cavalry appeared from somewhere, and rode slowly past our camping-place. Then long strings of yeomanry moved out in the direction we had taken when going towards El Auja. Thousands of camels passed carrying supplies for troops on our right flank. We were detailed to assist Australian and New Zealand engineers to dig for water at Bsani. We worked hard at night, and rested in nearby wadies during the day. When the engineers had no further use for us, we made roads, and pegged down miles of wire netting, wide enough for infantry to march four abreast. Still we did not complain. We knew that at last Allenby was going to strike, and we believed the dreary days of patrolling and attending to mange-infested camels was at an end.

The attack on Beersheba began at dawn on 30 October. With the light horse, London and Welsh infantry, and the artillery, we had moved forward under cover of darkness, and the early hours of morning saw us within striking distance of the ancient city of Abraham. The rumbling of the big guns, and the crashing of shells bursting on the sides of the hills was music to our ears after the long dreary weeks we had waited for something to happen. We waited for orders to move into action but they did not come. So far as the appearance of our camp was concerned this day was no different from any other during the months that had passed. It was grim irony that while the big guns thundered away towards the left of Gaza, and our infantry, and mounted horsemen were advancing on Beersheba we remained in camp and plastered our camels with mange-dressing.

"A damned insult!" snorted Jimmy Moore. If Allenby thinks he is going to shift the Turks without the assistance of the Camel Corps he will soon wake up to the fact that it cannot be done."

"He's keeping us in reserve," muttered another Camelier. "But take it from me we'll be there when there's some real fighting to be done."

The Cameliers watched much of the fighting from a distance. Before the sun rose in the east most of the barbed-wire entanglements south of Beersheba had been destroyed by our guns, yet in places sufficient was left to cause considerable inconvenience to the Londoners when they charged during the early morning hours and captured the enemy's advanced position. Now our guns were brought forward at the gallop, and at shorter range blew away what wire still remained.

The enemy artillery were now doing considerable damage so far as our positions were concerned. The gunners had the range and they knew every yard of the ground at which they were directing their fire. Still the infantry moved forward.

Fine men were these Tommies. Not one of them faltered as their long khaki lines advanced over the uneven ground. They worthily upheld the traditions of England's fighting men in other wars. The Turks were cutting gaps in their ranks with machine-gun and rifle-fire, and the ground over which they had advanced was dotted with dead and wounded.

Then the infantry got at close quarters, and with wild yells they charged the Turkish trenches. There was some fierce bayonet work. One burly Londoner, finding himself short of ammunition, gripped his rifle by the red-hot barrel with both hands, and swinging it around his head put several Turks out of action. He was a giant berserk; the pity of it is that just when the remaining Turks turned to flee he fell with a machine-gun bullet through his head.

While the infantry were moving forward our cavalry had advanced a considerable distance unseen by the enemy. Now they urged their horses forward and charged Tel el Saba, which was strongly fortified by the enemy. This was the highest point in the hills surrounding Beersheba, and many men fell while advancing upon it. For hours the Turks resisted every attempt to capture this position; it was not until late in the afternoon that it fell into our hands.

Beersheba was still held by the Turks, and the day was drawing to a close. The position was serious. Many of our mounted troops had ridden over thirty miles the previous night, and after moving all day the horses needed water. If the town, with its wells, was not captured before dark there would have to be a retirement so that the animals could be watered.

The sun was casting lengthening shadows when a great cloud of dust rose on the eastern side of Beersheba, and out of it came the 4th Light Horse Brigade to take the town. Never before in the history of warfare was a more desperate enterprise undertaken and carried to a successful issue. Using their rifles, with bayonets fixed, as lances they galloped over trenches, rifle-pits, and any of the enemy who dared oppose them, then raced on into the centre of the town. The Turks were too astonished to offer much resistance. In a few minutes hundreds of the enemy were killed, and nearly two thousand surrendered. A dozen guns and much ammunition also fell into our hands.

When darkness settled over the battlefield our troops were in possession of Beersheba with its precious water-supply. Soon thousands of horses were being watered at the wells where Abraham and his family once procured water for their flock. Clouds of dust still hung over the town, while men on horse and foot moved warily as mines and infernal machines were everywhere. Men who stopped to pick up shining coins, tins of tobacco and preserved meats were blown to fragments.

Now the Cameliers moved forward. The 4th Battalion rode away into the barren hills to the north of Beersheba. No. 11 and No. 14 Companies, with full supplies of food and water, followed them. Slowly they rode through the captured town, the camels picking their way between dead men and horses. No. 12 Company still waited for orders to move forward. Smelling of mange-dressing, and feeling somewhat disappointed that all the other camel companies on that front were on the move while our services did not seem to be required, we rolled into our blankets and slept. Perhaps we would not have slept so soundly had we known what was in store for us within the next few days.

The Cameliers to the north of Beersheba rode along rough mountain tracks and down rocky gorges, watching all the time for scattered bands of Turks who were fleeing toward the hills. At the same time they protected the flanks of the horsemen and infantry who were also moving northwards. Early on the morning of 1 November long lines of infantry marched towards Towal Abu Jerwal, and the Cameliers rode on the right of them. They were light-hearted, and as the camels took long sweeping strides over the rough ground their riders laughed and jested with each other.

"We don't know where we're going but we're on our way," said a Camelier.

"Yes," drawled another. "And when we get to Jerusalem I'm going to send my rich aunt back in Sydney a piece of the cross on which they crucified Christ. She will be so pleased when she gets it that she will mention me in her will."

An officer laughed. "You'll have no trouble in getting it. They sell them by the drayload in the Holy City. It must have been a darned big cross, as they have been selling pieces of it for about the last two thousand years."

Idle chatter, but it helped to pass the time. Although they were now "touring the Holy Land" as the Cameliers termed it, there was hard fighting ahead. The enemy were on the run from Beersheba to Gaza, but sooner or later they would make a determined stand, and the Cameliers would get their share of the fighting that would follow.

The Turks now showed signs of making a determined stand at Tel el Khuweilfe; reserves were hastened towards this stronghold from Beersheba and Gaza. On the evening of 3 November No. 12 Company were ordered to saddle their camels and stand by ready to move at any moment.

"This is where we are going to get what's coming to us," said Jimmy Moore, as he leaned over the saddle of his barraked camel. No notice was taken of him, but Jimmy liked to talk, and he always succeeded in persuading others to talk back to him. Looking around the Cameliers, who were either saddling or standing by their camels waiting for orders to move, his eyes rested on Frank Matzonas, who had just drawn a "pull-through" from the barrel of his rifle.

"Getting your pop-gun ready to mop up the Turks?" inquired Jimmy.

Matzonas nodded, and slung his rifle along the side of his saddle. Perhaps he was just a little "windy." With three years in the A.I.F., this would be his first taste of actual fighting. Most men were somewhat nervy at such a time.

An interesting character was Frank Matzonas. Born at Riga, now the capital of Latvia, he was assisting his brother to grow coffee in Java when the war started. He decided to spend a holiday in Sydney, but the day he arrived in that city he was walking along a main thoroughfare when he met a Russian in an A.I.F. uniform. The Russian taunted Matzonas for not enlisting. The next morning he presented himself at Victoria Barracks, and the same day marched into the training-camp at Liverpool. A clever linguist, he could speak German, French, and English besides his native language, and when he arrived in Egypt at the latter end of 1915 Intelligence claimed him for a time. Later he was cook at an officers' mess, but was eventually transferred to the Imperial Camel Corps. He came to No. 12 Company just after the second disastrous attack on Gaza.

It was not until an hour before midnight that we received orders to ride toward Beersheba, and at eleven o'clock the following day we passed through the ancient town, on our way to Tel el Khuweilfe. We now had a new leader in Captain Leslie Bell, but the Cameliers, never short of a nickname for a popular officer, generally referred to him as "Ding Dong." We were sorry to lose Lieutenant Jock Davidson, who had so gallantly led us during the last Gaza battle, but another unit claimed him.

Chapter 17

To the fighting horsemen Tel el Khuweilfe meant an abundant supply of water; and this was why that strongly fortified Turkish stronghold had to be captured at any cost. Looking at the barren country over which the Cameliers now travelled, we could well understand why the retreating Turks had imagined they would not be pursued by our troops. There was hardly a blade of grass on the plains. Here and there were miserable stunted, dust-covered shrubs, but they were soon tramped down by horse and camel. Ahead were barren hills with not a scrap of vegetation to cover the age-worn boulders.

We rode through clouds of dust that almost blinded and choked us. We were not sorry when we came to higher ground and left the dust-clouds behind, although the camels moved more slowly over the stony tracks.

Tel el Khuweilfe was an ideal spot for a fighting-force to resist the advances of an attacking body of troops. The enemy had cut trenches and machine-gun sangars all over the sides and along the crest of a flat-topped hill, on either side of which were forbidding ranges. The Tommies and light horse began the first attack, but were beaten back, and their lines were swept with shell-fire. There was no shortage of guns behind the enemy lines, and at times the air fairly screeched with shells. The light horse returned across the low hills to the left until they were within a few hundred yards of the main Turkish positions. That night the enemy tried desperately to wipe them out with machine-gun and rifle-fire, but the light horsemen took advantage of the scattered rocks and boulders.

The following morning another light horse regiment worked their way over a rugged ridge to the east of Khuweilfe, then on foot they raced across open ground swept by rifle and machine-gun fire. Reaching an area surrounded with boulders they also took shelter, and remained there all day. Turkish snipers had the ground covered, and the Australians lost several officers and men.

Early next morning many of the light horsemen were withdrawn after having repulsed counter-attacks by the enemy. They had been without food and water for over thirty hours, and were worn out for want of sleep. The 4th Battalion of the Camel Corps were now on the right of the Welsh infantry, at what was known as the Ras el Negh sector. On the 5th, with other mounted troops, they were ordered to hold the line while the infantry made an attempt to capture the Turkish positions to the south-west of Khuweilfe.

Meanwhile, the 3rd Battalion of the Camel Corps were riding through the Dhaheriye hills. The tracks over these were strewn with signs of a routed army— damaged rifles, ammunition, doctors' equipment, and German aluminium water-bottles. The Cameliers took a fancy to the water-bottles, and slung them across their shoulders. It was not always easy to get a drink of water from a fantass when travelling, and from that time onwards water was also carried in these handy and light German bottles.

As we advanced one of our planes appeared over a ridge, flying low, and making such a noise that we thought it was a warning that the enemy were concealed near by. We halted and sent an advance party ahead, but there was no sign of man or beast. Coming to a well we decided to dismount and refill our fantasses. Since we left Beersheba we had shared with thirsty light horsemen and Tommies much of the water that should have lasted us for another two or three days. Despite a warning that we would have to use our supply of water sparingly we could not refuse the requests of our thirsty comrades.

However, we were not to get water at this well. Seeing this was our intention, Major Nobbs ordered us to ride on:

"You have three days' supply or you should have," he shouted.

"What do you think of that!" muttered Jimmy Moore. "I reckon it's a fair cow we cannot get water when it's staring us in the face."

"It might be infested with cholera germs," said Frank Matzonas.

"Just as well to go out to it with a germ as a bullet, or a bomb, or a blanky lump of shell," replied Moore, as he cast another glance over his shoulder at the well.

Some distance ahead we came to another well. There were several surly-faced and filthily-clad Bedouins standing near it. Again we halted, but the Bedouins told us the well was dry. We did not believe them. Receiving permission from our officers to dismount we decided to investigate for ourselves. One of our men climbed down a rope leading into the depth, and came to a drive in the side of the well. There was clear, cool water at the bottom of the drive. It was a clever dodge cutting that drive in the side of the well. It appeared to be dry and a stone, thrown, struck the hard bottom. Probably that drive had been cut in the dim past when other invading armies passed this way.

Although there was more than sufficient water in the well for our requirements we were again ordered not to touch it. We then passed between barren gorges until we came to a flat ridge. There we halted. Outposts were placed on the summit of the ridge, and men were detailed to take the camels (excepting two) back to Beersheba, under cover of darkness, for water. The remainder of the men rested at the base of the ridge. During the night some of them went to the well with the drive and filled their fantasses. Next morning they were sorry. Diarrhoea began to trouble them, and during the strenuous days that followed most of them were sick men.

On our left the big guns were booming at intervals throughout the night. Just as we were preparing breakfast an enemy plane came flying low over the hills and opened a machinegun on the men lining the ridge. Our Lewis gunners got busy, but we had many narrow escapes from the bullets coming from above. No doubt the two camels in the valley below had attracted the attention of the keen-eyed German aviators. The machine flew about a mile in a southerly direction, then came back and presented us with more bullets. By this time we were concealed behind rocks and in crevices at the bottom of the ridge. Once again our Lewis gunners opened up, and the plane above swayed, then descended slowly, falling to the ground half a mile away.

After breakfast the camels returned with water, and we rode all day along rocky paths and between steep hills. Late in the afternoon we came within striking distance of Khuweilfe, and were told to rest as we would move into action at four a.m. next day. We rested, but few of us had any sleep, although we were not disturbed during the night. There was an occasional spitting of rifle-fire and the rattle of machine-guns. Away on our right we heard a man calling for stretcher-bearers, and nearer at hand someone uttered a string of oaths as he tripped over a stone and fell sprawling on his face. Lieutenant-Colonel de Lancey Forth walked in and out amongst us most of the night. Sometimes he stopped to speak to a few men seated in a group. We liked to see the tall, wiry Camelier hero of Gaza amongst us. He still carried a cane in his hand; I don't think he was ever without it when in action.

"How are you, boys?" he asked of several of us.

We assured him we would feel more comfortable, and perhaps get some sleep if he would go over to the Turkish trenches and tell the blighters to keep their infernal machine-guns quiet.

The colonel chuckled. "Won't be long now, boys. Nice little scrap in a few hours' time. It will be all over in a few minutes."

Away he went, still swinging that cane, to stop somewhere else and speak to another group. A remarkable man! Fear was foreign to him, and he had a kind word for every man in his battalion. The Camel Corps were fortunate in having brave officers to lead them. During the time I was with this unique fighting force I never heard of one officer in any of the companies who showed the slightest sign of fear when in action.

It was still dark when we received the order to advance. Moving slowly forward in artillery formation we crossed a rise, then down a hollow on the opposite side until we almost walked on top of a Turkish trench. We were immediately ordered to retire. Then a funny thing happened. Every man turned on his heel and walked back; and not a sound came from the Turkish trench. But when we found cover behind a low ridge the enemy sprang into activity, and a devastating machine-gun fire swept the ground over which we had just walked. The Welsh infantry were charging their positions to the left of us. Right into the enemy redoubts they went, but a counter-attack drove them back. Here the bayonet fighting was of the fiercest and most desperate kind.

We marched for about half a mile, then received the order to turn in a half right direction. Now the Turks turned their machine-guns on us, and we began to lose men. We went on for another quarter of a mile when we were ordered to lie down and make the best of things until daylight. We took advantage of what shelter was offering, and our casualties were light.

Just as the first rays of the morning sun peered over the horizon we were ordered to charge the enemy trenches to the front of us, but had not advanced far when we were ordered to dig in.

The remnants of the Welsh infantry who had been driven back from the Turkish redoubts, now began to fall back in disorder from portion of the ridge they had held for some time. Without a moment's hesitation Lieutenant E. W. Dixon, waving his hat, rushed towards them.

"Go back and hang on at all costs; the Camel Corps are on your right," he yelled. They stopped, listened to the wild-eyed Australian, then dashed back to the ridge they had just abandoned.

Then a heavy mist came floating over the enemy redoubts, and a few seconds later we could not see them.

"Gas!" yelled someone.

" Get your masks on!" cried another.

Under cover of the mist the Turks left their trenches and advanced close enough to hurl hand-grenades among us. We couldn't see anything a yard in front of us. Still, we peppered the mist. When it lifted the Turks had returned to their trenches.

Another hour passed. Suddenly there was wild cheering all along the camel lines. Behind, the 2nd Light Horse Brigade Machine Gun Squadron were racing towards us. The machine-gunners got their guns up a rise to within fifty yards of the enemy's first-line trenches, but paid a heavy toll. Here they remained all day, and their presence on the ridge gave us considerable relief as they now drew much of the Turks' machine-gun fire.

Considerable activity in the Turkish trenches set us on the alert for a counter-attack. Then Sergeant Dan Pollard shouted: "Cripes, they are all off to Constantinople with hats in their hands." Those were his last words. A bullet went through his head. Almost at the same moment Sergeant Arthur Oxford, while raising his rifle to fire, fell forward on his face. A bullet had entered the side of his nose, and he died without a murmur. Frank Matzonas pushed his head up from behind the little shelter in front of him, and got a bullet through his brain.

The machine-gunners on the rise were getting in some good work, but we sadly watched them dropping round their guns. Hell! It was hard to lie there and see them being slowly wiped out.

A doctor on a camel came slowly towards us, holding his medical pannier in front of him.

Down went the camel, shot in the hindquarters, but the doctor jumped from its back before it stumbled to the ground. Then picking up his pannier he came towards us. Without a word he began to attend to the wounded.

A string of water-laden camels led by Gyppos came over a rise. The Turks began to shoot them down, and terror-stricken and screaming the Gyppos fled in all directions.

The Turkish snipers above us were evidently picked marksmen. A Camelier's hat hopped in the air as a bullet ploughed a glancing furrow in his scalp. Another man had the stocks of three rifles shattered in his hands, yet was not injured.

Night's dark shadows crept up the valley; the enemy's firing slackened, and some of us slept. Some time in the night water was brought to us, and many of the wounded were taken away in cacolets.

Many times during the night we wondered how the light horse machine-gunners were doing. The sound of their guns had died down until we could only hear one firing at lengthy intervals. At last it stopped firing. When daylight came we saw they had gone, having retired during the early hours of morning, taking their wounded with them.

Reg Reid, of No. 12 Company machine-gunners, was sent to the rear for spare parts. Returning, he could not, in the dark, locate his unit. At last he wandered into a Turkish trench where he was bayoneted, and stripped of his clothes.

While walking about in the dark Lieutenant C. H. Lyon was shot dead, and Lieutenant Kessels was badly wounded. Snowy Darr, of No. 17 Company, was lying out in front of his unit. During a charge earlier in the day he had been unable to return with the other men. After dark he came back to his company and reported that Sergeant Findley was out in front, shot through the knee. Sergeant George Towner, Sergeant Morris, and Darr went out and carried him back to the lines.

Another Camelier named Neilsen lay wounded in the open for several hours, close to the Turkish trenches. Each time he called out the Turks put a bullet into him until he was riddled with them. Murderous beggars were those Turks who lined the heights of Tel el Khuweilfe.

When dawn broke camels were still carrying away the wounded, and the Turks began to, snipe them. It made us boil to see camels, cacolets, and the wounded inside them crash to the ground. In one cacolet were "Yank" Bell, and a trooper from the 2nd Light Horse Machine Gun Squadron. Bell had been awarded a Military Medal for bravery during the second attack on Gaza, and the decoration had been handed to him just before we went to Khuweilfe. It was in his upper tunic pocket when he was on the ridge the previous day, and a bullet went through it, then entered his body under the armpit. Trooper Stubbs of No. 13 Company, was urging the camel ahead by hitting it with his hat, when it was shot. He managed to get the two wounded men out of the cacolet, but could do no more.

Back on the ridge we watched Stubbs's plight. Someone had to go to his assistance. Trooper McGillivery dashed across the open ground, but just as he reached the dead camel he spun round and fell. We thought he was dead; but ten minutes later he began to crawl slowly towards the other side of the camel, where he was concealed from the Turkish snipers. Later when stretcher-bearers picked him up they found that a bullet had fractured one of his legs.

Most of the second day we still lay out on the slope of the ridge. Suddenly Lieutenant E. W. Dixon jumped up and cried, "If you are Australians follow me." Away he went with the Cameliers close behind. When we reached the summit of the ridge we found that the main body of Turks had retired. Their snipers had sacrificed themselves by keeping up a rapid fire to make the retirement a success. All were killed. Two of them lay behind each sangar. Remembering how they had fired on our wounded earlier in the day we gave no mercy, and I doubt if they expected it.

In the snipers' sangars we found several of the Lewis guns we had lost during the second attack on Gaza. The Turks had tried to use them against us, but evidently could do little with them, as they were jammed with bullets. Turkish bullets, having no rim on them, had become fastened in the drums.

So far as the Cameliers were concerned their casualties had been heavy. During the two days' fighting at Khuweilfe many splendid officers and men were killed. No. 11 Company were grief-stricken over the death of Captain Creswell. A son of

Rear-Admiral Sir William R. Creswell, he was a Gallipoli veteran, and an original member of the Camel Corps. The men in his company were greatly attached to him. Despite his rank he mixed with them as one of themselves. I remember one occasion when he had been away from his company for some time. Returning unexpectedly to El Arish one day, when several of his men were at the rail-head, a hard-faced unshaven Camelier went up to him as he stepped out of a carriage.

"Hullo, captain," he said, "where the blazes have you been?"

Creswell smiled. "Where have I been? Cairo, of course, and I've had a hell of a good time."

A group of Tommies, standing near by, were amazed at the familiarity between the Camelier officer and a private in his company.

"By goom," said one of them, "if we talked to our officers like that we would be in the blinkin' clink before we knew where we were."

On another occasion half a dozen men in his company had managed to secure a case of whisky, and in the lines that night they "let their heads go," finishing up with a free fight. Next morning they were paraded before Captain Creswell, each of them expecting nothing less than twenty-eight days in Abbassia jail. Creswell listened to what they had to say, and there was a hard, set look on his face rarely seen there. At last he picked up the crime-sheets in front of him and tore them into pieces.

"Damn it all, men," he said, "I can't crime you. We have been in some tight corners together, and not one of you ever squibbed. You are better fighters than drinkers. Go back to your lines, and if you drink whisky, behave like men, not like beasts."

There were tears in the eyes of many Cameliers when the body of Captain Creswell was carried away for burial.

When the Cameliers lined up and prepared to leave Tel el Khuweilfe, not one company had fifty men left. They had added to their laurels as a fighting force.

Chapter 18

After Khuweilfe we rested, and then with reinforcements we rode northward through Palestine. Gaza had fallen, and the Turks retired after doing all the damage that was possible to the water-supply. Weeks passed before our engineers had the wells in working order again.

The enemy were now a routed army. During the next two weeks our pursuit never slackened. Hard behind the Turks came the Anzac horsemen, yeomanry, and infantry. Few men amongst the pursuers could relate a connected story of what happened, or where it happened. Mounted regiments urged their horses ahead day and night. The Turks resisted at intervals, then fled to another point, where they again made a stand until shifted at the point of the bayonet.

This is a story of the Cameliers, so I shall relate our own adventures. The Camel companies now became scattered. Our battalion followed the light horsemen, and came to where a railway bridge had been destroyed by explosives. Rails and stones were scattered about everywhere. Here there was a large Turkish marquee hospital crowded with wounded and dead Turks. We went inside. Some of the Turks raised their hands to their lips, indicating that they wanted water. There was such a pleading look in their eyes that we gave them what water we could spare. Their clothing was filthy and their faces covered with blood and dirt. Judging by their appearances water had not touched their bodies for months. A bearded Turk lying on a blood-soaked stretcher feebly raised a hand and pointed toward me:

"Gallipoli?" he muttered.

I nodded.

"Good," he said, almost in a whisper.

That settled it. I could not refuse to help a Turk who had fought against us on the Peninsula. Taking them all round they played the game, which was more than I could say about some of their countrymen who were opposing us in Palestine. I lifted the filthy blanket covering him and saw his right knee was shattered. He would lose his leg when he was taken to one of our hospitals, but procuring some water I washed the horrible wound. Then I put a cigarette between his lips, placed a lighted match to it, and he puffed away contentedly. Patting him on the shoulder I turned to leave the tent.

"Australia good," were his parting words.

Another Turk with a fractured leg had crawled outside the marquee to find water, but was too weak to return. He lay beside a smashed ammunition-wagon, his leg covered with swarms of flies. A burly Camelier picked him up in his arms and carried him inside the tent.

We found a good supply of water and filled our fantasses, which were almost empty. It cheered us to know we had sufficient water in our tanks to last us several days, but we pitied those horsemen of ours ahead who did not ride with a fantass of water slung along the side of their saddles. Still, we gave as much of the precious fluid as we could spare when we met any of them. Just now they were doing all the dashed fighting, and they were entitled to the water.

We could not get wood to make a fire. Near by was a clump of Australian ironbarks; we were surprised the Turks had not chopped them down for firewood. Probably they had a reason for leaving them standing. There were no dead limbs on them. One Camelier snapped the stocks from some damaged rifles he found by the side of the road and made a fire, round which we all crowded to boil our billies. These were generally empty fruit-tins with a piece of wire for a handle.

Leaving the destroyed bridge, we swung along a track that skirted rugged ranges and came to signs of a big fight that had taken place the previous day. Dead Tommies and Turks were lying everywhere. Lying beside the road was a filthy-clad Bedouin, and as we passed him he moved slightly to avoid a camel.

The Camelier pulled up his animal and rode round the man. He did not move again. The camel stopped, lowered his head, then kicked the Bedouin in the back. With a yell he jumped to his feet and raced away. A roar of laughter ran along the Camel lines. The Bedouin was probably one of many who followed the battlefields to loot and to rob the dead. Afraid he would be accused of taking part in this ghoulish work, and shot by the Cameliers, he had pretended to be dead.

Farther along ammunition-carts, field-kitchens, and other vehicles were heaped in hopeless confusion. Horses and mules still harnessed to wagons loaded with ammunition, had been shot when they could go no farther. Teams of bullocks harnessed to wagons were also shot. This spot was literally a charnel-house; it sickened us to look at it.

On 13 November, with the yeomanry on our right, we advanced towards Yebna. We expected the Turks to put up a stiff resistance here, but they retired during the night, leaving us to enter the village without firing a shot. Wasting no time we rode on to the Wady es Surar, where we were placed as supports to the yeomanry, who charged the Turks much as the light horsemen had at Beersheba. It was a wonderful charge at the gallop in the face of a terrific fire from 5-9s and machine-guns. The guns were captured, and the Austrians handling them refusing to retire, were cut down.

Prisoners taken by the yeomanry were handed over to us, and many of the Cameliers claimed their belt-buckles as souvenirs. Dangerous things to carry: if the men with them fell into the hands of the Turks they could expect no mercy. Next morning we transferred the prisoners to the infantry, and rode onward.

Then came rain. Soon we were riding through quagmires of mud, while the camels slipped and often fell with their riders.

That night it was impossible to light fires and make tea, so we ate bully-beef and biscuits washed down with cold water, then slept on the soaked ground while rain pelted down on us.

We now swung towards the Mediterranean, still guarding the New Zealanders' left flank. Over a wide front extending inland, the mounted men and infantry were everywhere keeping the Turks on the move. With light hearts they rode and marched north-westward across the Philistine Plain, through villages with names famous in ancient history, and modern Jewish colonies where the inhabitants cheered our troops as they entered the villages.

We generally passed orchards at night. At such times orders drifted along the line of moving Cameliers that no man was to dismount. By the time the order reached the end of the line the men had jumped from their camels, and were in the orchards filling their saddlebags with large ripe oranges. The fruit was a luxury after weeks of bully-beef and biscuits.

Approaching Ludd we were able to buy brown bread from the Jews. They also sold us cut-up tobacco. Some of the Cameliers said any man who could smoke a pipeful of it was a hero. It had a frightful smell, and the only way to keep it alight was to smoke beside a fire with a blazing stick handy. All the matches in Palestine would not have kept a pipeful of the green weed alight when on the move.

One day we came to a field where a Bedouin was minding a flock of sheep. He knew by the looks on our unshaven and dirty faces that we were going to take them, so he presented them to us. That night we dined on mutton-chops and brown bread. After tea we sat back and informed each other that things could be much worse than they were. They were certainly worse next day when officers collected our pay-books and entered in them a fine amounting to two days' pay, for the mutton we had enjoyed the previous evening.

Halting for a brief spell at Surafend, a long, lean Camelier with a week's growth of beard on his unwashed face came over to our lines to see me. He was no other than Snowy Allen. I had not heard anything concerning him since he passed me on a cacolet-laden camel during the second attack on Gaza.

"Cripes, I thought they had sent you back to Australia."

He grinned. "No such luck. You've got to have an arm, leg, or head off before they'll send you back home. I tried every dodge. Swallowed soap pills, acted looney, and pretended I couldn't sleep. For a time the insomnia stunt had them thinking, but at last they must have woke up to the fact I was swinging the lead. I never was a good actor. As soon as I'd go to sleep at night a pimply-faced orderly would come along and wake me. 'Here,' he would say, 'matron says you've got to drink this.' Don't know what was in the glass, but it was sour enough to give Cleopatra's washerwoman the jim-jams. That went on every time I dozed off, and after standing it for two nights I asked the vet to send me back to my unit, and here I am. Landed back just before we moved from Beersheba. Suppose you haven't got a spare razor on you?"

"I should have thought you would have got things like that when you were in hospital."

"I did, my boy. I got everything that was to be got in the way of gifts. You never saw such a splendid collection in any soldier's kit. I'm in the Convalescent Hospital at Abbassia, and a couple of days before I was to return to this unholy land I had all those things spread out on my bed—razor, strop, brush, soap, shirts, and umpteen other things. Just then along comes an Irish regular, who is unfit for further service in the field. A hard case, he used to get a lot of free beer from our fellows. He stood beside my bed and gazed at the things spread out on it."

"Then stole them when your back was turned."

"Wait a minute. He looked at those things, and he told me if I wanted to turn them into cash there was a Gyppo shopkeeper outside the gates who would buy them. 'You could get a lot of beer in the canteen for the price those things would bring,' he said. I told him no Gyppo was going to get them if I knew it, and with that he went away. I had to go into Cairo that morning, and when I returned to the hospital there was my Irish friend waiting for me at the gate.

"'Come over to the canteen and have a drink,' he said.

"We had a drink, and after that we had many more. At last that old Mons hero, with the perpetual grin on his hard face, leaned close to me and whispered, 'That was good beer, wasn't it?' I told him it was so good in fact that nothing would please me better than to have some more. 'Sorry,' he said, 'but my money is finished. You see, I pawned those things of yours with that Gyppo when you went to Cairo. But I didn't spend one piastre of the money I got for them until you returned. Me lad, you 've been drinking your own money.' Now you will understand why I am looking for a razor to remove these two-inch bristles from my face."

Good old Snowy! As I listened to him my thoughts went back to the day when he pleaded with the Duke of Westminster to open the canteen at Mersa Matruh. That seemed years ago! Many of the men who were with us then were now under the sands of Sinai and Palestine. Snowy and I were still going strong, but I wondered how long the luck would last.

There was Bob Lloyd. He had fought on the Peninsula and was an original Camelier. Riding towards Beersheba he seemed disappointed. "Frank," he said, "I'm fed up with it all; after the next stunt I'm going to get a cushy job somehow." The next stunt was his last. The Turks shot him down at Khuweilfe. There were not many Gallipoli men left in the Camel Corps now. Yesterday I had spoken for a few minutes to Major Oliver Hogue about those old Gallipoli men. He was one of them, and one of the finest fellows who wore an A.I.F. uniform. A journalist on the staff of the Sydney *Morning Herald* before the war, and the author of two successful books written when he was at Anzac, there was no swank about Oliver. The Cameliers had a lot of time for him, and they went to him with their troubles. He was another of the Gallipoli veterans in the Camel Corps who did not see his homeland again.

I handed Snowy my razor and left him shaving. It was an issue razor that reminded me of a miniature crosscut saw when dragged over a bearded face. I did not like to see a good soldier in agony, so I went across to the lines to see if ticks were troubling my camel. When I returned he had gone back to his company.

The Bing Boys left us for a time and did fine work with the yeomanry around Latron. There the country was so rugged that it was impossible to wheel guns along the mountain tracks. However, the Bing Boys, with guns on their sturdy animals kept up with the fighting men slowly working their way toward Jerusalem.

On 22 November we moved to a point two miles south of Jaffa, and camped close to the 2nd Light Horse Brigade. Here we lay in supports for two days, and during this time our patrols extended out towards Ludd, which, according to legend, contains the tomb of St George. The Turks were now strongly entrenched between Yehudiyeh and Hill 265. We felt that at any moment we would go into action again.

Chapter 19

Ask an Australian who fought in the Great War what is his opinion of the New Zealanders, and he will most certainly declare that as fighting men they were superior to the men of the A.I.F. Put the same question to a man who served with the N.Z.E.F. and he will assure you that the Australians were more reckless fighters than themselves. Sizing them up in every way during those long months of strife: as fighters and all-round good fellows they were equal. The Camel Corps were fortunate in having in their ranks many heroic fighting men from New Zealand. In the vicinity of Jaffa they showed what they could do when in a tight corner.

In the early hours of 25 November the Turks advanced upon the New Zealand mounted men supporting the infantry at the Hadrah crossing. At this time another regiment of New Zealanders attacked the enemy's right flank, but the Turks put up such a vigorous resistance that they were compelled to retire, and the Turks entrenched themselves on Khurbet Hadrah.

There was now considerable activity all along the line. Still moving forward, assisted by their guns, the Turks forced the infantry and New Zealanders to retire to Jerisheh. Moving forward slowly, and yelling "Allah! Allah!" the Turks came to the Wady Auja. Here they stopped and directed their attention to the Cameliers who were holding "Bald Hill," or Hill 265 as it was known prior to this engagement.

The Cameliers were now so heavily shelled by the enemy's 4-2s that it was a wonder there were not more casualties in our ranks. Some of the men saw humour in the screeching shells as they came towards the hill: "Here's another; bob down, you're spotted," one man would yell. Another would reply: "Yes, and it's got your number on it."

At noon the Turks began to advance towards the New Zealand companies of the Camel Corps on the summit of the hill, and they had the advantage of dense prickly-pear hedge cover and a heavy artillery bombardment. After losing many men, the Turks took the hill where they dug in.

Later in the day the remaining companies of the 4th Battalion were ordered to move up to the assistance of their New Zealand comrades. Captain Howard and Lieutenant Jones of No. 18 Company were in charge of them. The other companies advanced on the left. It was dark when these men went up the ridge, and they were told to have something to eat as they would charge the hill at eight o'clock.

Brigadier-General Smith was ordered to retake the hill with the whole Camel Corps Brigade. The New Zealand companies were particularly anxious to meet the Turks with the bayonet. On the summit above many of their men were lying dead, and they wanted a chance to avenge them. With a look in their eyes that meant a bad time for anyone opposing them, they eagerly waited the order to charge.

The Turks began to move towards us, and one of our men called out, "Mind, they've got grenades!" With that we charged. The Cameliers were now grim and silent, intent upon the business confronting them. There was a moment of silence— then the two forces met. Men thrust and parried and gasped, and fell. Few of the Turks escaped. The New Zealanders were madmen; they bayoneted every Turk who faced them. It was the first time the Cameliers had a fair chance to use the bayonet, and they made the most of it. The Turkish front lines were broken almost immediately, and the Cameliers were again in possession of the position from which they had retired earlier in the day.

We held the captured trenches for half an hour, then again charged with the bayonet Turks entrenched on our left. They retired. Evidently they had no desire to again meet the Cameliers at close quarters.

When daylight came we had a further example of the nefarious practices adopted by the Turks—or their German masters. To the bodies of the dead New Zealand Cameliers they had attached devilish contraptions in the shape of bombs, so that when the dead men were moved, those near them would be blown to pieces. Fortunately none of the bodies were touched before these hellish contrivances were noticed.

Turks were now entrenched everywhere ahead of us with snipers posted in well-concealed sangars. A bullet from one of them hit the parapet behind which men belonging to the 18th Company were entrenched, and ricochetting struck Vic Coleman in the temple.

" I'm hit," he cried, as he fell backwards.

Corporal Hurst went to his assistance and started to dress the wound. A copper-coated bullet was sticking in the flesh, and the corporal withdrew it.

"Give it to me, and I'll keep it as a souvenir," said Coleman.

The bullet was handed to him and he placed it in his tunic pocket. He declared he could walk to the dressing-station, but another Camelier went with him, Coleman clinging to him most of the way. We did not see him again; he died soon afterwards, and the bullet he wanted for a souvenir was buried with him. The Camelier who had assisted him to the dressing-station returned under heavy fire with rations, which were very acceptable as we had not tasted food since the previous evening.

Enemy taubes came over and dropped bombs on our position. What with shell-fire, snipers, and the whining explosives from above, we were in a tight corner, and were not sorry when we were relieved. Marching to the rear, we had gone only a short distance when we were ordered to occupy a line of deserted trenches encircling an olive grove. Here the enemy shell-fire did not annoy us so much; their planes, however, continued to drop an occasional bomb near our trenches.

Ahead of us were several Camelier signallers frantically digging in to secure shelter from the enemy gunfire. At last they hacked out a trench deep enough to conceal themselves from the enemy. Shell after shell burst over their trench, and seeing no movement from it we thought the signallers were all dead. Probably the Austrian gunners had formed the same opinion as they transferred their fire from the signallers' trench, and began shelling ours. We also lay low, and the enemy gunners again transferred their fire to another quarter. We stood up and stretched our cramped limbs. Above the trench burrowed by the signallers rose a grinning face followed by others.

"Abdul is quite annoyed, isn't he?" yelled a signaller.

"Yes, and whatever is wrong with him he is blaming us for it," one of our men replied.

We all laughed. It was good to laugh again.

Those Austrian gunners were responsible for many casualties amongst the Cameliers in the vicinity of Bald Hill. Up there near the summit lay Sergeant Chard, his head almost blown to fragments. A game fighter, he had fallen while leading a small band of advancing Cameliers. There would be many fine men missing after this fight.

We again went back a short distance and dug in. Here we met No. 13 Company moving up to the front line. The Turks shelled us at intervals, and taubes also dropped a few bombs near our trenches. Still they did not do much harm as we had dug concealed trenches, i.e. what dirt we threw up was covered with grass, and it was difficult for the German flying men to locate our exact whereabouts.

We watched Lieutenant Hallam riding towards us from the direction of a provision-dump in the rear, which was being heavily shelled. He dismounted near our trenches and was about to fasten his horse to a stake when a shell burst overhead and killed him. The horse trotted away, and an Arab who was standing near by escaped without a scratch.

There were many of these Arabs roaming in the vicinity of

Bald Hill; when we asked them what they were doing they generally told us they were searching for cattle. We always sent them back to the rear to join other prisoners. They were spying on our movements. If given a chance they would find their way to the Turkish lines under cover of darkness, and relate what they had seen. We would have taken a greater pleasure in shooting some of them than in trying to wipe out the Turks in front of us.

A plane came flying low in our direction. When we saw the rings under its wings we took no further notice of it for some time. It flew low over our artillery positions and dropped smoke signals. A few seconds later the Austrian gunners sent across several shells which burst over our guns. It wasn't playing the game; but the army leaders opposed to us didn't worry about things like that. Our planes soon came in sight and drove the enemy machine behind the Turkish lines. We would have been better pleased had they shot it down.

We had left our camels in a patch of prickly pear a mile to the rear of where we were now entrenched. The enemy gunners began to shell them. Several of our men were detailed to remove the animals, and take them where they could be watered. The well was in charge of a native who appeared to be an Arab, and the water was brought to the surface with the aid of a suction gas plant. The first lot of camels were watered without any difficulty, then something went wrong with the engine. Mobs of camels were still coming to the well and soon they were barraked all round it. Sergeant Fred Barton told some of the Cameliers he didn't like the look of things, and that he was doubtful if the native in charge of the well was really an Arab. Barton looked closer at him, then expressed an opinion he was a Turk. Sergeant Ted Roardin produced a revolver and told the native if the pump was not working in ten minutes he would shoot him dead. Within five minutes it was bringing sufficient water to the surface for the thirsty animals' requirements. Had it not been for Roardin's threat no doubt the native would have made an excuse to go for something to repair the pump, and then have found his way to the enemy trenches, when the Austrian gunners would have shelled the hundreds of animals congregated around the well.

On the night of the 28th the 3rd Battalion relieved the 4th in the front line, and their machine-gunners continued sniping tactics until morning. The following night our men again charged the Turkish trenches with fixed bayonets, and on this occasion we were supported by a squadron of the 8th Light Horse. They were great fighters those light horsemen, and with their assistance we scattered the Turks.

A Turk fell wounded, but as he lay on the ground he raised his rifle to fire at one of our men racing ahead; a dirty trick, for which the Turks were noted. A Camelier coming behind noticed his action, but not having a rifle he took a running kick at his head. The wounded man fell forward; then, calmly stooping down, the Camelier wiped portion of the Turk's brains from his boot with a tuft of grass torn from the ground.

The 16th Company (New Zealanders) swept everything before them in a rush toward the summit of the hill where the Turks were entrenched. The Turks threw scores of hand-grenades amongst their advancing ranks and many fell. Chasing the Turks from the summit of the hill, they returned bringing their wounded with them. The following day General Smith and de Lancey Forth visited us, and warmly congratulated the Cameliers for the way they had held the Turks back during the past few days.

During the afternoon of 1 December the Turks shelled us heavily, and thinking they were preparing to advance No. 17 and No. 18 companies raided their positions, but suffered many casualties. Two days later a rumour passed along our lines that we were to be relieved and sent back to Rafa. We did not believe it. We had been fighting almost continuously for eleven days, and during that time we had not even removed the saddles from the backs of our camels. To make matters worse for the animals there was scarcely any fodder to feed them.

Late the same evening we were told the camels were being brought up to take us back. Now we really did believe the rumour. Just as the camels came up the Turkish guns again gave us a heavy shelling. They must have had some idea we were going to move. Six Cameliers were sitting side by side in a trench giving each other a light from a cigarette when a shell burst overhead. Every second man was killed and those in between were not injured.

Mounting we rode through mud for three miles, rain falling all the time. We were cold, and shivered in our sodden clothes. Not a man spoke. Many of the camels had no riders. Those who should have been in the saddles were lying in shallow graves back on the summit of the shell-swept hill, or were on their way to hospital.

Chapter 20

That night we threw ourselves down on a sandy ridge near the village of Yebna and tried to sleep in wet clothes and soaked blankets. Near by was an old Turkish aerodrome which had been wrecked by our bombing planes. All manner of debris was scattered about the village, showing how hurriedly the enemy had departed.

The following morning Trooper Cropper was cleaning his rifle when he accidentally shot himself in the knee. Later the leg had to be amputated.

That evening we again rode through mud and slush, with the rain pouring down in torrents. The camels had our sympathy. Mud was not their element. They slipped and slid and fell. Some of them fractured their legs and had to be shot. Bread brought to us by our transports was unfit to eat, so we went without supper. When we halted for the night we stood and shivered in the rain. Weary of standing we threw ourselves down in the mud and lay there. After considerable trouble the transport managed to light a fire and made cocoa. Rain had damaged the sugar, so we drank the cocoa without it.

When we moved away next morning it was still raining. Our camels continued to slip on the muddy tracks. When the poor brutes fell their lips would hang leeringly down, and one corner would droop just as if the animals were broken-hearted. Then, with many grunts and deep-throated noises they would throw their heads back in angry remonstrance as their riders tried to make them rise again. Suddenly they would lurch backwards and forwards, and try to get on their feet, only to slip and again flop in the mud.

By the side of the road Jimmy Moore was seated on a part of

an abandoned gun-carriage, and his camel was sprawled on its side in a pool of water.

"There you are," he said, when an officer rode over to him. "There's my camel, my rifle, and my ammunition. Anyone can have the blanky lot in exchange for a diving-suit."

"Things could be much worse," said the officer.

"Yes, if I was having a nightmare," grunted Moore, as he rose and tried to persuade the animal to stand on its feet.

Rain and cold are the camel's worst enemies. Some of the Cameliers became so disgusted that they left the animals lying in the mud, and walked along on foot. Then men were detailed to remain behind and urge the camels on again. Those that could not travel were shot, and their gear stacked by the side of the road.

The rain followed us to Rafa and then it stopped. "We also stopped, and camped. It was grand to be able to rest where there was no rain, mud, shells, taubes, or death. We washed our mud-caked clothes and indulged in sea-bathing. There were periods when we even forgot about the war. Then the usual rumours began to circulate. Those who thought they knew said that as the camels were useless in the Judean hills, we were to go back and patrol the banks of the Suez Canal. Others declared we were to proceed to Arabia, and link up with King Feisal's dusky troops.

Although the horrors of war did not trouble us for a time, we fell victims to an epidemic of camel itch; there were days and nights when we did little else than scratch the afflicted parts of our bodies. Instead of bathing in the sea we derived more relief from washing ourselves with phenyl diluted water.

Jimmy Moore put so much energy into scratching his itching legs that they were soon covered with septic sores. Then he was sent in a hospital train to Cairo. He told me all about that trip when he returned.

"I was asleep when the train arrived at Kantara," he said. "Suddenly I awoke and there was a woman bending over me. Blow me if I didn't think I was dead and that she was an angel. It seemed years since I had gazed on the face of an Australian girl. She handed me cigarettes, and matches, and a shirt—the first shirt I had worn for ages. I'm as rough as they make 'em, but I nearly cried when she smiled at me. Yes, she was Miss McPhillamy, who assists Mrs Chisholm to run the Soldiers' Rest at Kantara."

All troops who passed through Kantara and Jerusalem during the dark days of the late war were delighted when they heard that these two noble women had been decorated with the order of the British Empire. They did not find it easy to start their first canteen at Kantara, but once it was established on a solid footing it was a home from home for every soldier, no matter what rank he held, who entered through its doors. There was always a smile and a few words of greeting from the two fine Australian ladies who were in charge of it.

One afternoon our old fighting comrades, the Bing Boys, joined us. Covered with dust, and on camels that moved wearily, they came riding into camp as unconcerned as you like, and there was still a grin on their dusky faces. Since we last rode together they had shared in the fighting around El Burj, and their mountain guns had much to do with the victory that came our way on that lofty fighting ground.

The Bing Boys were also victims of camel itch, but they made good use of phenyl until they got rid of the distressing complaint. The Gyppo camel attendants attached to each battalion, not over clean in their habits, had the itch worse than any of us, and were given special treatment. They didn't like it. Their clothes were steam-disinfected, and naked as the day they were born each man had to get into a tank containing a lysol solution. A hole about five feet deep and twenty feet square was dug in the sand, and covered with a tarpaulin. When water was poured into the canvas it conformed to the shape of the hole. No doubt it was the first, and the only, bath most of these Gyppos ever had. Some needed a good deal of persuasion before entering the water.

One morning I strolled across to the canvas tank while the Gyppos were being forced into it. Here I again met Mick Burke, who had just pushed one of the natives into the lysol-diluted water. The Gyppo went in head first, and much of the water went down his throat. Spluttering and coughing he scrambled out of the tank and raced away in the direction of his camel-lines. Seeing me Mick laughed.

"Makes a fellow think he's back home," he said. "Reminds me of a mob of tick-infested cattle being driven through a dip."

The 1st Battalion, that had left the Palestine front after the second attack on Gaza, now returned from the Canal. Their arrival convinced us we were not yet finished with the firing-line, otherwise they would have remained beside the Canal until we joined them. It was not long before we received other reminders that there was further fighting ahead of us. One day we handed over our five-gallon fantasses, and in place of them we were issued with a second water-bottle. We underwent special training, and were never allowed to be idle for any length of time lest we got soft and out of condition for the strenuous days ahead.

Christmas Day was spent at Rafa, but there was little difference between it and any other day behind the firing-line. On New Year's Day each of us was issued with a frozen rabbit, that had once gambolled over some squatter's acres back in the land we Australians would have given a year's military pay to see again.

Shortly after this the 3rd Battalion proceeded by train to Kantara, then travelled to Ferry Post, where they began to patrol the Asiatic side of the Canal. As Cameliers their fighting-days were finished. When they again rode into Palestine they had became a part of the 15th Regiment of the Australian Light Horse.

Probably with the intention of making us forget all about the war it was decided to hold another sports meeting. The 1st, 2nd, and 4th battalions and the Bing Boys took a keen interest in it; all collected prizes. The most amusing events were the camel races. There is no course too large for a camel. Once they left the starting-place they were liable to do all sorts of remarkable things. They would begin by zigzagging over the desert sand, then finish with a great spurt, perhaps in the middle of the spectators. A fine upstanding brute, the property of Lieutenant Conrick, was favourite for the leading race. When the event started the animal bolted in the opposite direction, and scores of Cameliers wailed over the money they had lost through backing him.

The leading event of the day was the tug-of-war between the Bing Boys and the Cameliers. In previous meetings held at El Arish and Rafa, the Indians had collected the prize, but on this occasion the Cameliers considered they had some hefty men who would reverse the previous decisions. It was a strenuous struggle, but once again the Bing Boys were declared the winners.

Soon after the third sports meeting of the Camel Corps Brigade, we again received orders to move. We did not like it. Most of us had made ourselves very comfortable in this camp at Rafa, and we were beginning to enjoy the peaceful days there. We moved out with full marching rations for men and camels.

We camped in the vicinity of Tel el Fara, the second of the great boundary hills built by the Crusaders near Shellal. There were now many new men in the different companies, but few of the old originals. Some of the reinforcements were anxious to see a "bit of fighting:" the veterans were silent. As Mick Burke said, when we watered our camels in the wady: "The luck cannot last. Sooner or later we'll get skittled."

Burke was the last of the old mates of the training days at Abbassia. Snowy Allen and Jimmy Moore had gone back to the Canal with the 3rd Battalion. Mick and I would have been with them if we had not, in a foolish moment, transferred to other companies.

"Here I've been fighting and riding about the country ever

since we first left Abbassia," said Burke, "and the only decent break I've had was a few weeks in hospital after being so foolish as to experiment with a bottle of lice exterminator a Tommy gave me at El Arish."

I remembered that turn in hospital, but did not know the nature of the complaint that had taken Mick there. After much persuasion he told me all about it:

"It was this way: the lice had been chewing me to pieces, and I was sitting outside my bivvy, with my trousers in my hand, running a lighted match along the seams to roast the live stock, when a little Tommy came along and took a keen interest in what I was doing.

"'Be you killing chats, choom?' 'I told him I was not only killing them, but had already roasted a couple of thousand.

"'Well I'll be danged! My sweetheart back in Blighty sent me a bottle of something to kill them things. I'll give you some this afternoon.'

"No doubt that little chap meant well. I rubbed some of the stuff on places where the lice troubled me most. It took all the skin off the parts where I had rubbed it; then the flies got to work and they became septic. It must have been carbolic acid. I was in a nice mess and could hardly walk. I was afraid to parade to the M.O. in case he reckoned I had rubbed the stuff on to dodge the firing-line. At last I could stand it no longer and went on sick parade. When I told the M.O. all about it he believed me. Reckoned that no matter how windy a man was he doubted if he would adopt such drastic measures to dodge facing the Turks."

I suggested that the liquid should have been diluted with water, and Mick agreed with me.

"Anyhow, it put the kybosh on the lice," he said with a grin.

A few days later one of our officers made no secret of our destination:

"We're off to the Jordan Valley; and if I'm not mistaken there's a decent scrap at the end of the journey."

Once again we rode through Beersheba and over the Judean hills until we came to a wretched-looking village called Dhaheriye, on the Hebron road, now occupied by a few filthy-looking Arabs who scowled at us as we passed them.

"By cripes, by the look of the place it's entitled to its name," muttered a Camelier as he threw a couple of biscuits at a ragged urchin who was gazing with startled eyes at the long line of mounted camels.

Then over the wild hill-country where David had once wandered from Saul. On the hill-sides were ruins of ancient forts, and by the roadside wells with the brickwork on top worn by the ropes of ages. Descending gradually there appeared before us the towers and minarets of Hebron. High on the eastern heights of the town rose the long black walls and two stately minarets of a mosque which covers the Cave of Machpelah, the last resting-place of Abraham, Isaac, and Jacob.

Riding slowly over a wild, bleak hill we came to Bethlehem and rested. There was fighting ahead so we were given no opportunities to visit the Cave of the Nativity.

Good soldiers in action but hard cases out of it, the majority of the Cameliers were strangely silent as they rode past the birthplace of Christ. Few of them spoke as we neared Jerusalem.

Over bare limestone hills we came to the Jordan Valley, and camped near the modern Jericho. There was not much to see—a few huts and scattered shrubbery. I think most of us were disappointed. We remembered hearing in our childhood something about "Jericho, the city of Palms." There were no palms.

Chapter 21

Heavy rain had left the roads and tracks leading from the Jordan Valley in a wretched condition, and many of the paths stretching over the mountains of Moab were as slippery as glass. A muggy heat made the days and nights almost intolerable.

When the Turkish forces were driven from Jericho they destroyed the Ghoraniye bridge, and before our army could advance new crossings had to be made. The river was in flood, and a swift current made the engineers' work doubly difficult. At last Tommies swam the stream, beat back the Turks who tried to prevent their crossing, and assisted to pull rafts crowded with troops across the river. They worked under heavy fire from Turkish snipers, until they sealed the heights, shifted the snipers, then went back and assisted other men to cross the stream.

That little job occupied the best part of two days; then the troops prepared for the advance toward Amman. This was a strongly garrisoned town on the Hejaz Railway, thirty miles east of Jericho, and the Turks were determined to fight desperately before they would allow it to be taken from them.

On 22 March, after pushing the Turks from the high ground overlooking the Jordan, the 60th Division moved toward Shunet Nimrin. The Tommies were in high spirits and quite confident of success. They were delighted to be on the move again; anything was better than sweltering in the valley now below them. The Anzac horsemen and Cameliers rode out on the flanks; the artillery, ambulances, and supplies followed in the rear.

Enemy planes reported the movements of our troops. That gave the Turks time to prepare for our coming, and reinforcements were hurried from Damascus. We did not know this until prisoners supplied us with the information.

Marching through heavy mud, and climbing over rocks, some of them so steep that men had to stand on each other's shoulders, the Tommies eventually reached Shunet Nimrin, and drove the Turks back yard by yard. This without any assistance from our artillery, as it was impossible to bring the guns over the hilly country.

The road was now open toward the village of Es Salt, and the infantry again moved forward. Meanwhile the Cameliers were slowly working their way along rough mountain tracks and down steep gullies. So far we had not met any of the enemy, and it looked as if the Anzac horsemen and infantry would take Amman without our assistance.

The scenery never changed, and we were on a long trail with thousands of turnings. In whatever direction we looked there were rocks and huge boulders without a scrap of vegetation. Half an hour's silence was broken by a Camelier:

"A thousand acres of this blanky country wouldn't be worth one glass of Cairo beer."

"I'm darned if I know why the Jews reckon they want it back," said a sergeant in front.

"They might turn it into a quarry and make decent roads over these hills," said the first speaker.

Then the sky became overcast and it began to rain. Soon we were wet to the skin, and the camels began to slip. We covered half a mile in an hour when there was nothing to stop us. But there were many halts; when a camel slipped and fell, it took several men to get it on its feet again. At notoriously slippery spots the riders had to pave the quagmires with stones before the camels could get a footing. The language of the Cameliers was the most lurid ever heard in the Holy Land.

Some of the heavy transport camels carrying ammunition and supplies had worse experiences than the slim-legged animals we were riding. Some rolled down the steep sides of deep ravines and were not seen again. Usually the Gyppo drivers of the transport camels led two abreast; but on these goat tracks over the hills of Moab they had to travel most of the way in single file. Occasionally, probably out of pure cussedness, an animal loaded with ammunition would barrak in the middle of a path where there was a precipice on one side, and a dismal-looking abyss on the other. To flog the brute would, very likely, cause him to rear up violently, then stumble and go over into the abyss. So he had to be coaxed in soothing Arabic until he decided to proceed on his way.

At night, travelling over these slippery tracks was a hair-raising experience. Most of the Cameliers dismounted and led their animals—terribly slow going. Probably we didn't travel more than a mile during the night. Foot by foot we slipped and stumbled, afraid that at any moment the camel ahead would topple over a cliff. Every few minutes an animal would sway perilously on the edge of a precipice while the men in the rear would hold their breaths; then regaining its balance the camel would go on. The poor brutes were never meant for this kind of work.

After a lengthy silence a Camelier stumbled over a stone and into a pool of water.

"That settles it," he said. "As soon as this stunt is over I'll let the British army have my flamin' resignation."

The mirth of the Cameliers near him seemed strangely out of place amongst that long straggling line of gloomy, grumbling men.

When we came to Es Salt we found the Anzac horsemen and the infantry had taken it with little opposition. Owing to our late arrival, and the fact that they already had the Turks on the run, the horsemen and Tommies decided not to wait for us.

The infantry, covered with mud, and weary after marching for four days, were moving forward on the twenty-mile tramp that would bring them to the Turkish stronghold. Some exhausted stragglers assured us they would be in time to take part in the capture of Amman.

Accompanied by the 2nd Light Horse Brigade we rode through heavy rain, and shivered with cold as the night drew near. Many of the Cameliers went to sleep in their saddles. Nearing Amman we rested for twenty-four hours, as we had now been without sleep for three days and nights.

Not all of us had a chance to sleep. Some were detailed for outpost duty. A 1st Battalion trooper was amongst those doing outpost duty on the bank of a small creek. In an effort to dry his clothes he had removed them, and wearing nothing else but hat and boots was standing beside the stream when a Bedouin crept up on the opposite bank and fired at him. The bullet plonked in the water a few inches from where the Camelier was standing.

"By cripes, I'll fix you," he yelled, as he jumped into the water and waded across the stream, holding his rifle above his head. Reaching the opposite bank he dashed behind the shrubbery from which the shot had come. Wild shrieks and screams greeted him. He was amongst a crowd of Bedouin women and girls coming to the stream for water. Without hesitating the Camelier raced back to the creek, crossed, and dressed himself.

When the attack on Amman began we found ourselves operating in the centre, with Australian light horsemen and New Zealanders on either side. It was still impossible to bring up our heavy batteries, so the only artillery supports we had were the Bing Boys' mountain guns.

Before the attack we had been told that Amman was only garrisoned by a few hundred Turks. But in the past twenty-four hours reinforcements had been hurried into the town, and we now faced a force much stronger than ourselves. The enemy also had the advantage of ground; their positions could only be approached across a plain which was swept from end to end by rifle, machine-gun, and artillery fire. A dozen guns faced us from the heights of their most lofty position, known as Hill 3039.

We advanced over open ground, and for a time met little opposition. Then we prepared for the final dash. There was a nervous tightening of belts, an adjustment of bayonets, whispered words and facetious comments. Ahead of us the Turks, strongly entrenched in machine-gun pits and behind stone sangars, began to sweep our lines with machine-gun and shrapnel fire.

Early in the charge Trooper Trevaskis, of the 1st Battalion, got two bullets in the stomach. He fell near a dressing-station and within a few minutes an M.O. was attending to him. The doctor turned him on his back and began probing the wound. At last he declared he could feel a bullet or portion of one.

"Don't be damned silly," yelled the wounded man. "That's a piece of bone you are jerking about."

The M.O. inserted a pair of forceps into the wound, and catching hold of something solid tried to remove it. Trevaskis still swore and maintained the doctor was interfering with a bone, but when the forceps were withdrawn he had to admit it was a bullet. The wounded Camelier had a nightmare trip back to the Jordan in a swaying cacolet; but he recovered. Trevaskis was probably the only man wounded in the stomach at Amman who lived to return to Australia.

Meanwhile the 4th Battalion, in charge of Lieutenant-Colonel A. J. Mills had worked towards the Hejaz Railway, where they assisted in destroying Kissir Station; demolished several culverts and five miles of railway line; and then rode back towards Amman.

The Bing Boys plastered the Turkish trenches with their shells, but they were too light to do much damage. Later, after desperate efforts, a couple of batteries were brought up from the direction of Es Salt. They managed to keep the Turks quiet for a time, and continued our feeble bombardment after the Bing Boys ran short of shells.

Just before daylight on the third day we again charged the Turkish positions in front of Amman, and there was some desperate hand-to-hand fighting. A youthful Camelier in No. 4 Company went to fire at a Turk who was advancing upon him with a bayoneted rifle, but found he hadn't a bullet left. The Turk was on the point of bayoneting the lad when Paddy Bennington, of the same company, threw his rifle, butt first at him. The

Turk fell to the ground, and the lad promptly killed him with his own bayonet. Archie Searle, with five shots in rapid succession, killed five Turks.

A Scottie In No. 7 Company stumbled across three Turks working a machine-gun. Having lost his rifle in the charge he rushed them, swinging around his head a haversack containing two tins of meat. After being thumped over the head and shoulders with this unique weapon the three Turks threw up their arms and surrendered. Then, shouldering the machine-gun and driving his prisoners in front of him, the Scottie returned triumphant.

But after three days' desperate fighting we were unable to shift the enemy from their excellent defensive positions in the rocky hills.

The odds were too great, and we received orders to retire. Exhausted, sleepy, and shivering in our wet clothes, we moved back towards the Jordan. With heavy hearts we took a last glance at Amman. Many splendid officers and men had made the supreme sacrifice there. Amongst the dead Cameliers were Captain P. Newsam, Lieutenants Denham, Smith, Thorby, Sanderson and Adolph, at one time a well-known New Zealand footballer.

With the 2nd Light Horse Brigade in front of us we rode towards Shu net Nimrin. Drizzling rain was still falling, and we were so exhausted that we could hardly sit in the saddles. We had managed to get our wounded away; but as there were not sufficient cacolets for all of them, some were strapped to the backs of horses, and light horsemen walked and led the animals. Reaching Es Salt they were transferred to ambulances.

At Es Salt many of the Christian inhabitants who had rejoiced when our troops rode into the town, now decided to accompany us back to the Jordan, fearing that if they remained behind the Turks would kill them and outrage the women after their display of sympathy with the British force. Carrying such meagre belongings as they could collect in so short a time, aged men and women, children, and even babies joined in the procession. Some of the more fortunate of the refugees had horses and donkeys, but the majority just shouldered their bundles and walked. On the muddy mountain tracks many of the women and children became exhausted, then the horsemen placed them in front of their saddles, or in some instances gave them a horse to ride while they walked. Cameliers rode over the slippery ground with babies in their arms, while the mothers came behind. One mud-covered, unshaven Camelier held a three-year-old girl on his knees as the animal he was riding plodded slowly over the uneven ground, and was endeavouring to feed her with a biscuit that had been soaked in water at the last halting-place.

"Are you getting your hand in so that you'll know something about nursing when you go back to Australia?" asked another Camelier.

"Don't be silly. I've got half a dozen like this youngster running about Australia with tomahawks in their hands."

Another Camelier had taken a baby from its mother's arms, and was endeavouring to put it to sleep. In a husky, high-pitched voice he was crooning to it the half-remembered words of an old song:

Only a leaf, ah but what grief
It caused in the dim long ago.

The infant looked up into his dirt-grimed face and gurgled joyfully.

"Knows its blanky dad!" laughed the Camelier riding behind him.

"Yes, and you'll know the weight of a wallop on the jaw if I hop off this camel," was the reply.

In the rear Shana Khan, the best athlete in the Hong Kong and Singapore Battery had a footsore woman perched behind him, and the seat was far from comfortable. With her arms around his waist she clung desperately to the Indian.

A Camelier who had fallen out of the main line now rode past him in order to catch up to his comrades in front.

"By cripes, Shana, I'll write and tell your wife about this," he said, a wide grin spreading across his face.

175

Shana Khan and the Bing Boys near him laughed loudly.

Passing through the village of Mujahid many Bedouins joined the refugees. These nomads of the desert look upon their womenfolk as beasts of burden. Bowed down with heavy bundles on their backs the women walked wearily over the rough and slippery tracks while the men strolled behind them, never attempting to relieve the women of their weighty burdens. The Cameliers thought this over the odds; so they dismounted, and ordered the women to put their burdens on the ground. Their menfolk were then compelled to carry them and when they objected the Cameliers used their boots with such vigour that the scowling Arabs picked up the bundles, while their women had the unusual experience of following them unhampered.

There is no need to dwell on that awful ride back to the Jordan. It was worse than the journey towards Amman. On that occasion the Cameliers had ridden confident that victory lay ahead; now they were returning worn-out and defeated. That was what hurt. Somehow they did not understand why the Turks could not be driven from the heights of Amman.

On the eleventh day after the commencement of the raid the Cameliers returned to the Jordan Valley. Some of the camels had not had the saddles off their backs for eight days. The transport camels, which had carried ammunition and supplies over the hills were in a worse plight. When the saddles were taken from their backs some of the flesh came away with them.

Chapter 22

The Cameliers rested in the Jordan Valley for a day and a night, and washed the mud of Moab from their clothes. Then leaving our camels behind we moved forward on foot and relieved the infantry on the western side of the valley. Here we occupied roughly-constructed trenches extending from Mellahah to Musallabeh. The Turks shelled us from a distance, and their planes, always soaring above, presented us at intervals with a liberal supply of bombs. But we soon dug in deep enough to prevent them causing many casualties in our ranks.

Musallabeh was the most prominent hill in our line. Abdul knew he would have to take it before he could make any sort of advance into the valley below. In front of this hill, which we occupied, was a deep ravine, and beyond it was the scrub-covered slopes of Green Hill. Farther to the north, and in a slightly westward direction lay Brown Hill, called by the Turks Beghalet. Beyond this hill rose mountainous ranges where the enemy had their guns cleverly concealed. From these mountains ran many shallow wadies which offered splendid shelter for the Turks when they decided to advance in our direction. Everything was in their favour to capture Musallabeh when they were prepared to strike.

In our rear the Hun airmen were giving our camels a bad time with bombs. Day after day they came across and shelled them, probably thinking the Cameliers were with them. They killed and injured a few of our animals, but their bombs created more havoc in the lines of the transport camels. During the time we lined the heights of Musallabeh over a hundred of these animals were put out of action by aerial bombs.

After one of these bombing raids word drifted to our lines

that a camel owned by a man named Lewis had been blown to fragments that morning. Lewis was seated in a trench when the news reached him.

"That's more than I can bear," he said, wiping imaginary tears from his eyes. "I rode that old camel all the way from the Canal, and I had high hopes of taking him back to Australia when the war finished."

"What were you going to do with him when you returned home?" asked another Camelier.

Lewis grinned. "Dunno. But at nights when I was sitting in the front room relating my war experiences to an admiring father and mother, not to mention half a dozen brothers and sisters, it would have been nice to have the old camel beside me, barraked on the linoleum. The smell of the old animal would have given a bit of colour to the hair-raising experiences I would relate."

It was hard digging in those trenches. Mostly clay and rock, and with a fierce sun pouring down upon them, the Cameliers swore and perspired. After the rain the mud dried in the valley below and changed to a fine powdery dust which rose in clouds at the slightest movement of man or beast. When a breeze came our way, we had dust with our meals and in our drinking-water, and our blankets were covered with it when we retired for the night.

Then came flies and mosquitoes. The flies showed a fondness for jam when we spread it on bread. In a few seconds a jam-covered slice of bread would be covered with them. Mick Burke reckoned they tasted better than the flies he had swallowed at Anzac. He admitted they were a smaller species, but more of them covered a slice of bread. At night mosquitoes gave us no rest.

Each day the Turks showed themselves in the distance, and when they did we expected the attack we knew was coming. We worked hard to make our position stronger. That was where Abdul slipped. Had he charged our positions when we first took over from the infantry he may have met with success. Guns were also brought up and concealed behind Musallabeh.

We got busy laying barbed wire, and working at night the Turks did not know where it was placed. That was a maze of death that was to cause them considerable surprise in the near future. We felt more confident when we saw those spiked entanglements ahead of us; they would hold an advancing force while we thinned their ranks with machine-gun and rifle-fire.

Waiting for the Turks to attack made us "jumpy." The slightest sound at night from the direction of the Turkish positions was the signal for us to jump to our feet and grip our rifles. German shock troops, it was rumoured, had been brought from Damascus for the coming attack—big powerful men who would hurl us back by sheer weight.

"Huh!" grunted Mick Burke. "Let 'em all come. The bigger they are the heavier they fall when they get a bayonet in the guts."

A mail was brought to us in the trenches. One Camelier read a letter, rolled it in a ball, then throwing it on the floor of the trench, stamped on it. A few moments later he picked it up again, spread it out on his knee, and read aloud portion of it for the benefit of anyone who cared to listen. We all listened.

"Me flamin' aunt," said the Camelier. "And this is what she says: 'You are indeed fortunate to be in the Holy Land, and I suppose by this time you are somewhere in the Jordan Valley, with its sacred and historic associations. I am sure you now spend much time reading the Bible I gave you when you left Australia. It will be more interesting now that you are actually seeing the places so often mentioned in it. I believe that portion of the ancient wall around Jericho can still be seen. Do bring back one wee stone from it and I will treasure it as a souvenir from that land of milk and honey, where you must now be having a very enjoyable time.'"

The Camelier again rolled the letter and tossed it out in front of the trench. Seeing the grin on our faces his wrath broke out afresh.

"Land of blasted milk and honey!" he roared. "And me having a very enjoyable time! Yes, covered with camel itch, smelling of stinking camel day and night, almost eaten alive with flies and mosquitoes, and likely to be knocked rotten any flamin' minute. I'm having a great time, my oath I am."

"Don't forget when you go back home to take a piece of the old Jericho wall with you," suggested someone.

"You bet your life I will. I'll take it back and if anyone mentions the Holy Land to me I'll brain them with it."

One night the Turks advanced some distance across the open ground in front of their positions. Their cries of "Allah! Allah!" sent the Lewis gunners rushing to their guns, and the rest of us lining the trenches and peering into the darkness.

"They'll want Allah to help them when they get here," muttered an officer.

One nervous finger pressed a trigger, and then others fired. Towards the left a couple of machine-guns drummed intermittently; then there was silence. We waited but nothing happened.

Somehow we were disappointed. We wished they had advanced. Waiting was getting on our nerves. We wanted them to charge and end the suspense.

Men who had been suddenly disturbed went back to their blankets, hoping this time they would not be aroused before morning. Others rested their rifles lightly on the parapets, then stooped down to light a cigarette.

In a trench to the right of us someone began to sing softly, "*Si Muero en la Carretera.*" How it caressed our ears!

"That's a fellow in the 4th Battalion," whispered someone. "Used to be in an opera company one time. I heard him sing that song one day in the Red Lion, opposite Shepheard's in Cairo. But I don't like to hear him singing it in this hell hole that might soon be covered with dead and dying men."

Daylight peered over the horizon. There was no sign of the Turks, but soon afterwards their guns began to shell our positions. One of their planes came across from behind the hills to the north, watched where the shells were falling, then went back the way it came.

Early next morning the enemy swept across to the attack.

Chapter 23

The early morning hours of 11 April were no different to any other morning so far as the men lining the summit of Mus-allabeh were concerned. In the distance we heard an occasional rifle-shot, where a sniper thought something was moving out in front. Then there was another interval of silence. It would soon be daylight, and we would then arouse those comrades of ours who were sleeping in the rear.

Then someone yelled "They're coming!" Men sprang to their feet, and rifle in hand, raced toward any shelter that was offering. Not for a second did their eyes leave those straggling, swift-moving lines of Turkish infantry out in front. With finger on trigger they waited for them to come closer.

They came within a hundred yards of the barbed-wire entanglements, then our light guns began to shell them. At the same time the light horsemen began to cut them down with rifle-fire. Some dashed forward, only to be held up by the barbed wire, and there shot down. Machine-guns clattered on both sides of us. Still, the enemy knew the country—every ravine, almost every boulder. They knew exactly which way to go to get out of sight, and when they judged that getting out of sight was in order, they lost no time about it.

At the barbed wire they seemed undecided what to do. They knew that once they tried to work their way through that maze with its cruel barbs, they would offer an excellent target for our keen-eyed riflemen. While they wavered the light horsemen began to enfilade them on the left. Urged on by German officers they again advanced, and brought up several machine-guns which began to pour a deadly hail of bullets towards the trenches in front of them. At the same time our Lewis gunners were sweeping their advancing lines.

We could now see that the Turks' main attack was directed toward that portion of Musallabeh known as "The Pimple," and held by the 1st and 4th Battalions of the Camel Corps. The 2nd Battalion was in reserve.

Once they were close enough to our trenches to throw hand-grenades, the Turks gave us the liveliest two hours we had experienced since we left the shores of the Canal. We hurled grenades at them, but were not so well supplied with the handy little bombs as were the Turks. Several Cameliers loosened boulders and rolled them down on the advancing men below. Apparently there were hundreds of them, and they were being skilfully led.

Lieutenant-Colonel Mills, Commander of the 4th Battalion, repeatedly stood in full view of the Turks, and shot several.

The Lewis gunners were having a frightful time. Four days before the attack on Musallabeh the gunners attached to No. 4 Company had taken up a position on the extreme left of the ridge. They were soon shelled out of it, and had to occupy another position a short distance away. These men were Garland, O'Rourke, Souter, Jackson and McAuliffe.

Three days later a machine-gunner from No. 2 Company crawled to No. 4 Company's gun section, and began to assist them. Later a Camelier named Brown joined them. Waiting for the attack they knew was coming, a shell burst above them, and when the dust lifted, the headless body of the No. 2 Company's gunner was lying beside them.

This death of the gunner for a while dumbfounded the others. Then another shell burst above them. Portion of it tore the flesh from Brown's back and mangled the upper part of his right thigh. Souter was almost cut in halves, and died without uttering a word. Brown was carried away to die soon afterwards.

That night Garland and McAuliffe were taken away suffering from shell-shock, leaving only Jackson and O'Rourke with the gun. O'Rourke asked for two more men, and they were sent to him later in the night.

When the enemy launched their big attack early the following morning the gun was put out of action by shell-fire, and O'Rourke was hit on the left arm with a shrapnel pellet. Dressing it the gunner ordered Jackson to proceed to the rear and get some spare parts for the gun.

The Turks were now close to where the machine-gunners were concealed. Jackson raised his rifle to fire at one, but the Turk was too quick for him. Raising his own rifle he shot Jackson through the head. Lying beside the damaged gun O'Rourke shot the Turk who had killed Jackson. Just about this time the two men who had been sent to reinforce the gunners the previous night were also killed, and O'Rourke was the only man left out of the team of seven. A Gallipoli sergeant, a corporal from No. 2 Company, and a bomb-thrower named McGrath now rushed forward to assist the lone machine-gunner. The sergeant, who had brought spare parts with him, now began to work the gun, but several Turks rushed forward to put it out of action. O'Rourke shot one of them, and McGrath killed the others with bombs.

O'Rourke's wound was troubling him, but he refused to leave his gun. He crawled beside the sergeant to relieve him when he wanted a rest. Several more Turks now rushed the gun, but, turning it in their direction, the sergeant killed four of them, while McGrath stopped the others with a few bombs. The three men with the gun now found themselves in a tight corner. The Turks were determined to put the gun out of action. One of them crawled forward, then hurled a stick bomb, but it did no harm, and the sergeant killed him. The other Turks now hesitated.

Somewhere behind the advanced line of Turks a sniper had been busy all morning; he was a splendid marksman, and had killed or wounded several Cameliers. Trooper A. Searle, of No. 4 Company, was now observing for the machine-gunners, and, seeing another Camelier creeping towards them, he warned him not to look over the top of the sangar. The Camelier ignored the warning, and the sniper shot him through the head. Another man now crept forward, and the sniper killed him. With several dead men lying round him, the sergeant still worked the gun, and laughed softly each time he dropped a Turk who tried to creep forward.

At this stage of the fighting some of the Cameliers stood in the open and rolled boulders down on the enemy.

It was an all-in fight. The men from headquarters were doing splendid work. "With supplies of bombs, they raced over open ground to the front line, delivered the grenades to those who badly needed them, and raced back for a further supply.

Our officers were splendid. Captain Mills, of No. 2 Company, fell wounded, and Lieutenant "Ranji" Nield was killed, while setting fine examples to their men.

After a little over two hours' furious fighting the attack weakened. The Turks on the slopes below were still sheltering behind anything that rose a few inches in front of them.

Towards midday there was a scarcity of water. In this respect the Turks were in a more desperate plight. Some of them foolishly exposed themselves while endeavouring to take a bottle from a dead man lying near by. Then keen-eyed Cameliers would lightly press the triggers, and other Turks would join those still forms scattered about the slopes.

Some men are remarkably humane on a battlefield. A Turk, dragging a shattered leg, crawled from behind a rock and tried to reach a water-bottle dropped by someone as he charged up the hill. A bullet hit a stone within a few inches of the wounded man's face. He stopped, held up his hand, then motioned with it towards his mouth. The Cameliers could not resist that pathetic appeal; he got the water-bottle, and not a shot was fired at him. Returning slowly to the rock that had sheltered him earlier in the day, he again raised his hand, probably as a gesture of thanks.

Just after midday, light horsemen rode out from the left flank, bent on getting round the enemy and capturing them. But the German leaders had considered such a move, and had entrenched their flanks, and many concealed machine-guns compelled the light horsemen to retire.

Frank O'Rourke, the machine-gunner of No. 4 Company, and the men assisting him, were still holding their ground. They were hungry, but just before midday someone gave O'Rourke a tin of bully-beef and biscuits. He placed them behind him, but a shell deprived him of a meal. When the shell blew the tin of meat and biscuits to fragments, O'Rourke turned to the man on the ground beside him:

''That gave me a hell of a fright,'' he said in a shaky voice.

The nerve-racking ordeal through which he had passed since the previous day was now beginning to tell on the heroic gunner. The only survivor of the original gun crew, he expected to be killed any minute.

Another shell came screeching through the air, and, bursting near where he was standing, lifted Lieutenant Mackenzie off the ground. Then the Turks started another barrage; and our artillery began to shell them as they advanced. Some of these shells were falling short, so between them and those fired at us from the Turkish guns the Cameliers were having a warm time. O'Rourke killed eight Turks. Food, water, and rum was now brought to O'Rourke and the men assisting him.

With the coming of darkness we strengthened our position. The 2nd Battalion of Cameliers were now brought from the rear to reinforce us. We also buried our dead.

The Turks continued to move about the wadies all night, and we expected another attack at dawn. "When it was light enough to see, we were surprised to find they had retired with their wounded. A few stragglers were pursued and captured by light horsemen.

Annoyed, apparently, at our stubborn resistance, the enemy shelled us at all hours of the day and night. Otherwise, everything was quiet amongst the hills where the Turks were concealed. If it had not been for the barking of their guns we would have thought they had retired many miles.

At this time the enemy were "windy." They knew the British would strike again, but did not know just where. Any activity on our part was sure to be followed by a visit from their planes and fierce shelling of our positions. Down in the valley the planes also continued to bomb the horse and camel-lines; we lost several animals, but, on the whole, our casualties were light.

One morning we received a visit from General Allenby. He warmly congratulated us on the way we had driven the enemy from the slopes of Musallabeh. He also informed us that the hill on which we had fought would in future be known as "The Camel's Hump."

When he left us, Mick Burke removed his hat, scratched his head, and said:

"I don't like it."

"Don't like what?" asked another Camelier.

"I don't like to hear Allenby telling us what great fighters we are. There's something behind it. I'll bet anyone here a day's pay to a tin of bully-beef that we are going into another big scrap. He's only giving us that garden stuff to cheer us up."

For once Burke was wrong. As Cameliers we had fought our last battle. Several days later we were officially informed that the Imperial Camel Corps was to be disbanded.

Chapter 24

Towards the end of April there was a heavy concentration of cavalry around Jericho. Then the infantry began to move, and the Anzac Mounted Division rode on their flanks. The Bing Boys went with them. They showed their white teeth in wide grins as they rode past us. They would have been annoyed if they had been left out of any fighting about to take place, and were never so happy as when they were shelling the Turks. There were new faces in the battery. Many who had fought with us at Gaza were dead, wounded, or had returned to their homes, unfit for further service.

We waited for orders.

The mounted troops rode north towards the Turkish road leading from Nablus to Es Salt. It was their intention to stop the retreat of the garrison at Shunet Nimrin after it was attacked by our infantry.

The infantry marched all night, and attacked during the early hours of next morning, but were compelled to fall back before a superior force. The light horsemen held back Turkish reinforcements, and at night they took up a position in a deep wady overlooking the Nab-lus-Es Salt road. Here men wheeled the guns over rough mountain tracks, while wagons and limbers were lowered down the steep sides by means of ropes. The horses managed to scramble down the rugged slopes.

The Turks were moving fast. They were aware, days previously, that the British were to make another attempt to capture Es Salt and Amman. At night they crossed the Jordan with the intention of closing in on the left flank of the light horsemen. Soon after dusk they attacked the men in the wady, and so heavily did they shell our guns that an attempt was made to remove them; but it was practically impossible to get horses to drag them up the steep banks. Four horses were harnessed to a gun. They hauled it up some distance, then slipped to the bottom in hopeless confusion. Men were no more successful. At last orders came to retire, and the guns had to be left behind.

It was the first occasion in the campaign when the Turks had captured British guns, and our men keenly felt their loss.

Some of us went to see the Bing Boys when they returned to the valley. They didn't say much about themselves, but light horsemen told us they had done wonderful work with their guns when our troops approached close to Es Salt. The Indians seemed greatly concerned at the loss of the guns manned by the Honourable Artillery Company and the Notts Battery.

"All the same, we win next time," said Shana Khan, as he left a group of inquisitive Cameliers and went to feed his camel.

We now lived under wretched conditions in the valley. Flies, mosquitoes, and scorpions did not give us a minute's peace. Scorpions found their way into any clothing lying about, and many of the Cameliers were stung by them when they rolled into their blankets. They were responsible for the deaths of several men in the infantry; others were sent to hospital with poisoned arms and legs. Still, they provided the Cameliers with a certain amount of amusement.

Many of the men staged scorpion combats in sand-encircled rings. Mick Burke became the owner of one that killed all the others matched against it. He called it Napoleon, and carried it about in a tobacco-tin. He won a considerable amount of money backing Napoleon.

One day Burke heard that a trooper in one of the light horse regiments had a scorpion he claimed to be the best fighter in the valley. He challenged the light horseman to a combat. The Cameliers backed their favourite with every piastre they had, while the light horsemen did likewise with their champion. When the gladiators met, Burke's scorpion was killed by its opponent, and grinning light horsemen collected our money.

In the valley, too, was a poisonous snake that had a fondness for blankets. So plentiful were these reptiles that when a man turned in for the night he realized he might not wake again. Many men, bivouacked on the banks of the Wady Auja, were bitten by snakes and died soon afterwards. Fringing both banks of this narrow stream were tangled scrubs which offered the reptiles a splendid place of concealment.

Men were encouraged to catch and kill them. One light horseman was quite an amateur snake-charmer. Hardly a day passed but he killed at least a dozen of the deadly reptiles. He exhibited his daily catch on a wire stretched between two shrubs.

Another man used to catch and place them around his arms, neck, and even inside the shirt he was wearing. One morning he caught a medium-sized specimen and placed it in an officer's nosebag, inside which was the officer's tin of tobacco. Soon afterwards the officer put his hand in to get the tobacco, and felt the reptile. With a yell he rushed to the M.O.'s tent.

"Quick, doctor," he cried. "I've been bitten on the hand by a snake."

The M.O. examined his hand, but failed to find where he had been bitten.

"But I felt the damned thing stick its fangs into my hand," persisted the officer. "And I'm a doomed man if you don't do something quick and lively."

The M.O. and several others decided to examine the nosebag. In the meantime the trooper had removed the snake and in its place left a small piece of rope. When the M.O. emptied the bag all that fell out of it was the piece of rope and the tin of tobacco.

Then along came the trooper with the snake coiled round his neck. This was too much for the officer. Turning to the M.O. he cried:

"For God's sake send me away for a spell, doctor. I 've got a touch of the dry horrors."

At this time Jerusalem was out of bounds, but parties of not more than twenty men each were issued with passes for a tour of inspection under the guidance of a padre. Such sacred spots as the Holy Sepulchre, Mosque of Omar, the Stations of the Cross, and other places were visited, and a short lecture was given by the padre at each place.

On one occasion, after several parties had been dismissed outside the Jaffa gate, a Tommy and a Jock began to discuss what they had seen. The Tommy said his padre had told them that the Romans killed Christ. The Jock replied that his padre told them the Jews had killed Him. To settle the argument that followed, both men agreed to approach a party of Cameliers, just dismissed, and ask their opinion.

"Well, I'm damned if I know who killed Christ," said one who had been asked to express an opinion. "But it's a flamin' good job the Cameliers were not here then, or they would have been blamed."

A few days after we had been told that the Imperial Camel Corps was to be disbanded, having outlived its usefulness so far as Palestine was concerned, an officer came along and asked all men to step forward who had transferred from the infantry to the Camel Corps when it was first formed. Very few stepped out. Many of them were dead; others had been invalided back to Australia.

"I cannot say for certain," replied the officer in answer to a dozen questions fired at him, "but I've an idea the infantry men in this Corps will rejoin their units in France."

The following day we were told that Lieutenant-Colonel T. E. Lawrence was going to G.H.Q. in Cairo to see if the four Camel Corps Battalions could be sent to Akaba to assist his Arab troops in their pursuit of the Turks on the left flank. We didn't like that rumour. Those of us who had patrolled the Libyan Desert during the early days of the Camel Corps activities knew what that would mean—sand-storms, long stretches without water, camel mange, and occasional skirmishes with the Turks.

"I reckon the best way to settle where we are going," said

Mick Burke, "is to get all the 'heads' together— Chauvel, Chaytor, Lawrence, and others who may want us, then put us up for auction, and the highest bidder takes the lot, with the Bing Boys chucked in for luck."

Every day brought a fresh rumour. At last we received definite information that three companies of the 2nd Battalion, in charge of Colonel Buxton, were to travel across Sinai, and join up with Lawrence's Arab army at Akaba.

Most of the camels were to be handed over to Lawrence. We were sorry for the camels. Although we had often cursed them, when they were to be taken away from us, we found that we had become quite attached to our ugly, ungainly mounts. The Arabs would not treat them as kindly as we had done, and we reckoned they were entitled to a long spell in country that suited them better than the rough and slippery mountain tracks of Palestine.

Then came a morning when we mounted our camels and rode from the Jordan Valley. Although we felt sure we would see it again we knew we would not ride through it on the backs of camels. In a few weeks' time the Imperial Camel Corps would only be a memory so far as the Australian, New Zealand, and Indian troops in it were concerned.

Chapter 25

The Cameliers stopped at the Jewish colony at Richon le Zion. The inhabitants of the pretty little village were extremely hospitable, and the Cameliers received a warm welcome. Richon was noted for its vine-growing industry, and the Cameliers declared the wine to be the best they had ever tasted. As some sampled it in large quantities, they were certainly in a position to know what they were talking about.

Our camels were now taken from us. This ending (so far as the Australians and New Zealanders were concerned) of the Imperial Camel Corps could not be allowed to pass without a ceremony to mark the occasion. It was decided to hold a funeral service: a camel-saddle, complete with all gear, was wrapped in a Union Jack, then carried outside the camp, where it was officially and ceremoniously buried.

There was nothing frivolous about the proceedings. Brigadier-General Smith referred to our hard-fighting career since the brigade had left Abbassia. The majority of the Cameliers, I am sorry to say, did not give him the hearing to which he was entitled. He was by no means an approachable man, and his manner did not tend to make him popular with the Dominion troops. The rank and file very rarely saw him. He was a good organizer rather than a personal leader. The smooth working of the brigade while it was in the field was a testimony to his organizing ability, and when the Cameliers were in action he skilfully carried out the instructions given him by the higher command. Holding the rank that he did he was not seen actually participating in any of the battles in which the men of the Imperial Camel Corps distinguished themselves.

No time was wasted in mounting many of the men on horses, and giving them the necessary drilling to enable them to become light horsemen. Others (many of them "hard cases") were sent to the Detail Camp at Moascar to receive riding instruction. They were a merry crowd as they marched, fully armed, into camp. At their head was the O.C. and several staff officers. The guard at the camp turned out and presented arms as the Cameliers approached. Only the officers and one of the leading sections had passed the saluting guard when a voice yelled:

"Dismiss the guard! We're only the flamin' Camel Corps."

During the weeks that followed many Cameliers sorely tried the patience of their instructors. They mounted their horses and fell off them again; they growled and grumbled, and declared that, as they would never even make apologies for light horsemen, they should be sent to reinforce the infantry in France.

Issued with leave passes to Cairo, they, as usual, got into trouble. At night some of them visited Ismailia and sampled the Egyptian rum, which Mick Burke declared was so fiery that one whiff of it would kill a man a hundred yards away. When they returned to camp they made their presence felt; their main grievance seemed to be that they would soon have to return to Palestine with its flies, scorpions, snakes, and dust-clouds.

Part of the camp instruction was riding on a wooden horse. The Australians, coming from a country noted for its horsemen, reckoned it was an insult. One night a Camelier, after a night in Ismailia, stumbled against a wooden horse, and immediately ordered it to barrak.

"You won't, eh?" yelled the Camelier. "Well, I'll damn soon make yer."

Next morning an agitated Tommy major wanted to know who had mutilated the wooden horse. The inebriated Camelier had borrowed the cook-house axe and chopped its four legs off.

"Anyhow, I made the blanky thing barrak," whispered the Camelier to his mates.

Their training completed, the ex-Cameliers again returned to Palestine. The Australians from the disbanded Corps became the 14th and 15th Light Horse Regiments, and later on a French colonial regiment of Spahis and Chasseurs d'Afrique were attached to them. The three regiments formed the 5th Australian Light Horse Brigade. Brigadier-General Macarthur Onslow was promoted from the command of the 7th Australian Light Horse Regiment, and took charge of the new unit.

The New Zealanders of the Camel Brigade became a machine-gun squadron, attached to the new brigade. The Bing Boys assisted them with their mountain guns. The Camel Corps Ambulance, mounted on horses, were also attached to the new light horse brigade.

The ex-Cameliers were just as much together as when they were in their late unit; old mates in the former different companies were not parted. And they still had the same officers. So it was not surprising that they continued to be a formidable fighting force until the end of the war.

The three companies of the 2nd Battalion were now all that remained of the Imperial Camel Corps. Colonel Lawrence at once arranged for them to ride from the Suez Canal to Akaba, and attack Mudowwara by night.

Mudowwara was a watering-station on the Damascus-Medina railway, and was garrisoned by about two hundred Turks with several machine-guns and four mountain howitzers. The Turks had constructed splendid trenches and many stone sangars for snipers.

The Cameliers intended to attack at 3.45 a.m., but in the darkness it was not easy to find the route over which they had to travel, and daylight was almost showing when, in three parties, they charged the Turkish positions. After bombing the front trenches they charged over them, many of the Turks surrendering without firing a shot. They were still dazed at the suddenness of the unexpected attack.

Colonel Buxton displayed skilful leadership at Mudowwara, and was one of the first of the attacking party to reach the trenches. Close behind him came Lord Winterton, who had joined up with the 2nd Battalion when it was first formed at Abbassia. Later on Lord Winterton transferred from the Camel Corps, and became one of Colonel Lawrence's staff.

Buxton's Cameliers continued to operate against the Hejaz Railway, south-east of the Dead Sea. Although they did not have any fighting worth mentioning they were always handy should their services be needed. When they were disbanded after the Armistice the Imperial Camel Corps ceased to exist.

Fifteen years ago! How time flies! Those veterans of the Imperial Camel Corps who rode over the scorching sands of the Libyian Desert, across the sandy wastes of Sinai, and into the Promised Land, are now scattered far and wide. Many have gone to meet their Camelier comrades who made the supreme sacrifice on the battlefields.

Brigadier-General C. L. Smith was a sick man during the closing days of the war, and died in England some years back. After the armistice Lieutenant-Colonel N. B. de Lancey Forth returned to his former unit, the Sudanese Camel Corps. He visited Australia in 1925, where he met many of the Cameliers who had served under him. He died in Alexandria, Egypt, on 1 March 1933. Major Oliver Hogue accompanied other Gallipoli veterans to England after the armistice, and died there, from pneumonia, soon after his arrival.

Wherever they are now—those veterans of the Imperial Camel Corps, with their one-time cheerful outlook on life, and their generous, improvident attitude—these days of depression must be hard for some of them. If there should be another war in our time, we would recognize many hard-bitten faces, with greying hair, all coming forward to have another "cut at the blighters."

ALSO FROM LEONAUR

AVAILABLE IN SOFTCOVER OR HARDCOVER WITH DUST JACKET

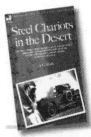

LEONAUR

ALSO FROM LEONAUR
AVAILABLE IN SOFTCOVER OR HARDCOVER WITH DUST JACKET

EW2 EYEWITNESS TO WAR SERIES
CAPTAIN OF THE 95th (Rifles) *by Jonathan Leach*
An officer of Wellington's Sharpshooters during the
Peninsular, South of France and Waterloo Campaigns
of the Napoleonic Wars.

SOFTCOVER : **ISBN 1-84677-001-7**
HARDCOVER : **ISBN 1-84677-016-5**

WFI THE WARFARE FICTION SERIES
NAPOLEONIC WAR STORIES
by Sir Arthur Quiller-Couch
Tales of soldiers, spies, battles & Sieges from the
Peninsular & Waterloo campaigns

SOFTCOVER : **ISBN 1-84677-003-3**
HARDCOVER : **ISBN 1-84677-014-9**

EWI EYEWITNESS TO WAR SERIES
RIFLEMAN COSTELLO *by Edward Costello*
The adventures of a soldier of the 95th (Rifles) in the Penin-
sular
& Waterloo Campaigns of the Napoleonic wars.

SOFTCOVER : **ISBN 1-84677-000-9**
HARDCOVER : **ISBN 1-84677-018-1**

MCI THE MILITARY COMMANDERS SERIES
JOURNALS OF ROBERT ROGERS OF THE
RANGERS *by Robert Rogers*
The exploits of Rogers & the Rangers in his own words
during 1755-1761 in the French & Indian War.

SOFTCOVER : **ISBN 1-84677-002-5**
HARDCOVER : **ISBN 1-84677-010-6**

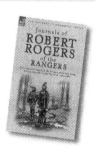

ALSO FROM LEONAUR
AVAILABLE IN SOFTCOVER OR HARDCOVER WITH DUST JACKET

SF1 CLASSIC SCIENCE FICTION SERIES
BEFORE ADAM & Other Stories
by Jack London

Volume 1 of The Collected Science Fiction & Fantasy of Jack London.

SOFTCOVER : **ISBN 1-84677-008-4**
HARDCOVER : **ISBN 1-84677-015-7**

SF2 CLASSIC SCIENCE FICTION SERIES
THE IRON HEEL & Other Stories
by Jack London

Volume 2 of The Collected Science Fiction & Fantasy of Jack London.

SOFTCOVER : **ISBN 1-84677-004-1**
HARDCOVER : **ISBN 1-84677-011-4**

SF3 CLASSIC SCIENCE FICTION SERIES
THE STAR ROVER & Other Stories
by Jack London

Volume 3 of The Collected Science Fiction & Fantasy of Jack London.

SOFTCOVER : **ISBN 1-84677-006-8**
HARDCOVER : **ISBN 1-84677-013-0**

WF1 THE WARFARE FICTION SERIES
NAPOLEONIC WAR STORIES
by Sir Arthur Quiller-Couch

Tales of soldiers, spies, battles & Sieges from the Peninsular & Waterloo campaigns

SOFTCOVER : **ISBN 1-84677-003-3**
HARDCOVER : **ISBN 1-84677-014-9**

Lightning Source UK Ltd.
Milton Keynes UK
UKHW01f0853020818
326666UK00001B/52/P